W9-DDN-719

My Life with Edgar Cayce

My Life with
EDGAR CAYCE

by David E. Kahn
as told to Will Oursler

Doubleday & Company, Inc., Garden City, New York
1970

Library of Congress Catalog Card Number 76–89071

Printed in the United States of America
First Edition

To
Cynthia, David, Beecher, Jason, Adam, and Alex,
my grandchildren

Preface

I did not know David Kahn until I began to work with him on this book. I met him first at a luncheon, arranged through a friend, to discuss the possibility of my assisting him in the preparation of a book about his long association with the world-famous prophet and psychic Edgar Cayce.

I found Kahn to be a man in his mid-seventies, full of an almost unbelievable exuberance and love of life, full of enthusiasm for Edgar Cayce and his achievements—and full of stories about American business giants and industrialists with whom Kahn, guided by Cayce, had been involved through many years of his active career.

Kahn was closer to Edgar Cayce and his family, over a longer span of years, than any other human being. He personally brought many individuals to Cayce for readings; he himself helped to take down hundreds of the readings in the early days. He knew Cayce as friend and fellow adventurer across the Texas prairies and oil fields—and ultimately into the jungle of New York City. But he knew his friend Cayce above all as an associate in psychic and metaphysical discovery.

David Kahn became an adventure in himself—garrulous,

amusing, beguiling, with a hundred stories of the great and near great in government, in the White House, in the Defense Department, in industry, in the Army, in medicine, in religion. Yet underneath all this was a depth of religious and personal meaning and searching for spiritual values and understanding.

As a journalist who likes to think of his beat as the universe itself, I agreed to work with him on this story of a tall, lanky, Bible-reading, nature-loving Southern fundamentalist—gifted with unique and seemingly inexplicable powers—and a young Jewish boy whose father operated a large wholesale and retail business in Lexington, Kentucky.

As a start, after organizing the basic material, as journalist and interviewer, I helped David Kahn put down the facts in his own words, on tape recordings. Our plan was to have these transcribed and then to reorganize and edit the material for final book publication.

Unfortunately, fate did not allow the complete fulfillment of this plan. But it is David Kahn's story nonetheless, told essentially as he told it.

I am deeply grateful to all who aided in the completion of this work, including especially David Kahn's charming and always cooperative wife, Lucille, with her patience and guidance and assistance at every point. And her magnificent courage and faith.

I am grateful equally to Hugh Lynn Cayce, to the Association for Research and Enlightenment at Virginia Beach, Gladys Davis Turner and the ARE staff, and to the many others who aided in the preparation of this book.

Their help has made it possible to present here what is—except for the last few chapters—David's story in David's words.

Will Oursler

Contents

My Life with Edgar Cayce

BOOK ONE

In the Time Before . . .

In France, Edgar Cayce had a dreamlike experience. He saw it many times, and it was essentially the same, even though it came to him with a variety of details. Sometimes the ultimate destination was a long and shadowed hall; sometimes it was a room without windows or doors, where a figure holds the Akashic records in the great book where all things, all deeds, all thoughts, of every human being are written.

And Cayce would recall, out of his dream:

"I see myself as a tiny dot out of my physical body, which lies inert before me. I find myself oppressed by darkness, and there is a feeling of terrific loneliness. . . . Suddenly, I am conscious of a white beam of light. As this tiny dot, I move upward following the light, knowing that I must follow it or be lost."

Or he would go another way:

". . . I passed into outer darkness, so dark that it actually hurt—yet there was a stream of light that I knew I must follow, and nothing on either side of the light must detract from my purpose to receive for that other what it was seeking in the way of aid for itself.

"As I passed along the line of light I became conscious of forms of movement crowding toward the light. Coming to the next plane (if we choose to call it such), I realized that the forms of movement or figures were taking shape as humans, but rather the exaggeration of human desires. Passing a little farther, these forms were gradually lost; still I had the consciousness that they were seeking the light—or more light. Then the figures gradually took form, continually coming toward the light.

"Finally I passed through a place where individuals appeared much as they are today—men and women—but satisfied with their position. This number of individuals in this state of satisfaction continued to grow, and then there were homes and cities where they were content to continue as they were.

"Still following the light, which grew stronger and stronger, I heard music in the beyond. Then there came a space where all was springtime, all was a-blossom, all was summer. Some were happy, some desired to remain, but many were pressing on and on to the place where there might be greater understanding, more light, more to be gained. Then I reached a place where I was seeking the records of lives of people that lived in the earth. . . ."

CHAPTER 1

A Neighbor Next Door

I was fifteen years old when I first met the tall, Lincolnesque man named Edgar Cayce. At that time we were living in a place called Hampton Court, in Lexington, Kentucky. We had just moved into this beautiful new twelve-room home—my father and mother and nine children. I was the oldest son. In that pre-supermarket era of the early 1900s, my father, Solomon Kahn, owned and operated a very successful group of grocery stores.

Soon after we moved into our new home, the William DeLaney family moved in next door. Mr. DeLaney had made a fortune in hardwood lumber. His wife had been terribly crippled in an automobile accident. Totally paralyzed, she was confined to a wheelchair and could not even lift her hands to comb her hair. They had a son seven or eight years old.

Mrs. DeLaney and my mother became good friends; my mother would visit with her and help her out in any way she could. Mr. DeLaney, we learned, had tried all over the world to help his wife find something or someone who could restore her health.

That we were devoutly Jewish, and they devout Roman

Catholics, in no way impeded our growing friendship, but it did play an important role in events relative to possible help for Mrs. DeLaney. These began one day when Mr. DeLaney said to me, "David, there's a man named Edgar Cayce in Hopkinsville, Kentucky. They claim he has psychic powers. They claim he does incredible things. I've telephoned him to come to Lexington to give a diagnosis—he calls it a reading—on the physical and mental condition of my wife."

Mr. DeLaney said this Cayce, whose regular business was photography, had agreed to come. But, he said, there was a serious problem in which I might be able to help. Roman Catholics were not supposed to deal with such people.

"I'd like to know if you would object to coming to our house when Mr. Cayce arrives, to cooperate with him and to take down the reading?"

I not only had no objection; I was thrilled. To me it sounded like a great adventure in an area of life which at that time I knew virtually nothing about at all.

Two days later, Edgar Cayce arrived in Lexington. To me he seemed quite old—in fact he was only thirty. It was in the cold months of the year; I believe December. Yet he had come all this way without an overcoat. I was tremendously impressed by this man. He looked like some backwoods Kentucky farmer, but I knew at once that he was much more. He had a kindly face, but it was his eyes that I noticed. They were grayish blue but the tone—even the color—seemed to change. At one moment you might almost think he was dreaming. Then you would feel those eyes seeing right through you. I felt this deep look when we first met. He was fair complexioned, and his face was long and thin. The cheekbones were high. He stood very erect, very slender, and spoke very deliberately. He told me he was in the photography business. His specialties, he said, were children and railroads. He seemed interested in me as a possible subject for future pictures.

When he walked into the house, Mr. DeLaney asked him if he wanted to see Mrs. DeLaney. Cayce said no, he preferred not to at that time. He wanted to give the reading first. Then he would meet her and see how closely the impression he got when he saw her fitted into the reading he gave.

I noticed that once or twice he said "we" instead of "I." Some time later, I asked him why he did this. Cayce said, "I—and the forces that give me this power—we work together."

He said that by himself he did nothing; he was simply a channel by which and through which the information flowed. That first day, before the reading, he gave me a black book with some suggestions neatly typed in it. I was to give him these suggestions, he said, at the proper time. He said that he would lie on his back, with his hands placed across his abdomen and his feet close together and he would look at the ceiling. I was then to say to him, "Now, Mr. Cayce, you are going to sleep. . . ."

Carefully he explained how I was to sit by him and say what was typed out in the book. Then when he said the words that would come at the end, "I am through . . . ready for questions . . ." I would ask for any questions Mr. DeLaney or his doctor felt they wanted answered.

The typing in the black book consisted of suggestions for putting him into what we would now describe as a hypnotic sleep, in which he could absolutely sever himself from his conscious mind and would have no awareness of his own words. After telling him that he was to go to sleep, I would say, "You will hear me and follow the suggestions that I make to you. Answer slowly and distinctly because I am writing in longhand." After this, I followed his instructions by saying, "Mr. Cayce, you are now at 58 Hampton Court in Apartment 1-A, in Lexington, Kentucky. Present in this room are Mr. William DeLaney, and Mrs. DeLaney's physician, and David E. Kahn. You will allow your mind to go to the rear of the apartment and there you will locate Mrs. DeLaney. When you have found her body you will go over it in great detail. Tell us any physical condition you find that might need correction."

I was, of course, a neophyte at this kind of thing. I followed his instructions precisely, giving the first suggestions just as his eyes were about to close. If the person giving the instructions waited even a few seconds beyond this point to give the order, Cayce would go into a natural sleep but would not be able to speak or to answer questions. Fundamentally, although there were minor changes and additions, the form of suggestion we used then was never changed in all the years and thousands of readings that followed.

The DeLaney reading was given on the floor of their living room; Cayce was simply too long for their sofa. I sat beside him with pads and pencils. Cayce in trance repeated each statement of mine; I wrote it all down, whatever he said or repeated.

After I gave the order to him to let his mind go to the back of the apartment, he said, "Yes, we have the body and mind of Mrs. DeLaney here." He proceeded then to go over her like a doctor, giving blood pressure and blood count and other physiological details.

Then—lying there on the living room floor in hypnotic sleep—he made the statement that the woman was a paralytic and he described her condition in medical detail. At Cayce's insistence, none of this information had been given to him by the husband when he called, neither the nature of her ailment nor the cause.

Still in trance, Cayce stated that the family had lived in Fort Thomas, Kentucky, and that Mrs. Delaney had been in a horse and buggy accident in which she had leaped from the surrey and struck the base of her spine against the step. He said that six or seven years later she had been in an automobile accident and that this second accident brought out the original injury. This combination of conditions brought on total paralysis.

As I wrote all this down in longhand, I recall that he used a number of words I did not know how to spell. When he used the term osteopath—the word was unfamiliar to me at that time—this largely unschooled Kentuckian asleep on the floor spelled the word precisely and explained what it meant. He said that one had just arrived in Lexington, a Dr. Barbee. There was no indication of how, having just arrived in the city himself, Cayce could know this obscure piece of information.

Still in sleep, he also gave a prescription for several medicines and mixtures which were to be taken internally.

After he had answered our questions, he said, "We are through for the present." I then gave the suggestion, "Now, Mr. Cayce, you've given an excellent description of Mrs. DeLaney's condition. Thoroughly relaxed and perfectly refreshed, without any ill effects of any kind from the condition of the patient whom you have discussed, within three minutes you will wake up."

I took out my watch and waited. Three minutes later, to the second, his eyes opened and with a little jerk of his head he sat up and asked, "How was the reading?"

I read back to him what he had said.

A moment later, Mrs. DeLaney came into the room in her wheelchair and Cayce met her for the first time. She was very heavy because she had spent so much time in the wheelchair. Only five foot five, she weighed two hundred pounds or more.

As soon as the reading was over, I hurried downtown with the prescription to one of Lexington's leading pharmacists. He did business with us—my father bought some of his patent medicines for resale in our stores. I told him to fill the prescriptions exactly as I had written them down. He didn't question them because there was nothing in them to cause him alarm.

Nevertheless, some days after she had taken the medicines, Mrs. DeLaney broke out in a rash from head to foot. Her physician indicated that he had been afraid something of this sort might happen. He said he could suggest nothing because he had no way of knowing which of the remedies had caused the rash.

Feeling deep responsibility, I sent a telegram to Cayce. I gave no information. I simply asked him to tell us the condition of Mrs. DeLaney now and to advise us. To answer, he would go into a trance reading which his wife would take down. In about two hours, a wire came back. The purport of its message: "If you will fill the prescriptions as given you will get the results promised the patient." It said further that if the massages, osteopathic treatments, and medicines suggested were taken, as directed, she would be able to resume her normal life. It stated that black sulphur, although a part of the prescription, was missing from the prescription made by the druggist.

This was Cayce's reply. I took the telegram down to the pharmacist. He said he had never heard of black sulphur. He got out the pharmacology and showed me that no such item as black sulphur was listed in it. So he had used regular sulphur.

I went back and asked Mr. DeLaney if I could wire Cayce again and ask him where we could find out about or get hold of black sulphur. We sent the telegram. The answer came back: Parke, Davis, Detroit, Michigan.

On receipt of this information, the pharmacist himself called the company in Detroit. They had the item, which was apparently new on the market, and they sent it. A few days after it was taken, the rash was gone.

For Mrs. DeLaney, Cayce's suggestions for treatment proved successful. The DeLaneys also located Dr. Barbee, who *had* just moved to Lexington. A short time after Mrs. DeLaney began osteopathic treatments, she was able to lift her arms, comb her hair, and feed herself. A few years later—just before I lost track of her—she was driving her own car, looked radiant, could get around on her own and, although not actually cured, could live to a considerable degree a normal life.

Some years later, William DeLaney appeared before Notary Public A. L. Meiler in Fayette County, Kentucky, and duly attested to the truth in the following statement:

"Mrs. DeLaney has been a sufferer for a number of years; and several years ago I heard of the ability of Dr. Cayce, and requested that he come to Lexington, which he did. He was the first to correctly diagnose Mrs. DeLaney's trouble; altho' she had been to a number of physicians throughout the country. . . .

"As a result of my acquaintance with Dr. Cayce in connection with this work; I have no hesitancy in saying, that he has wonderful hidden power. . . ."

It was signed by W. E. DeLaney.

For me, this was the beginning of what the future was to mean and involve. I was convinced that when Cayce in his hypnotic sleep made a statement it could be relied on. His answer to a question would be a right answer, if the question was asked properly; if not, you got an improper answer.

He told me then and repeated on many occasions, "I don't know anything about this, but I've been doing this work for a long time, and people tell me that I'm able to describe their conditions, and if they do what we say in the readings, they get results. If I ever find out that I give wrong information, or hurt anybody, or it doesn't work out, I'll never give another reading. But so far, I've been doing it ever since I was a little boy, and experiences with my family have taught me that if they can't be cured they can be helped. . . ."

For me, I had met a miracle man, I had seen him and heard him. And he was no fraud or demon-possessed force of evil. He was a human being with a human nature and all its virtues and failings. But a being who also had this other quality, this other psychic avenue, this other source, as if he could reach out to all knowledge and take at will what he required.

When the reading at the DeLaney's was over, I took Mr. Cayce next door to our home to meet my mother and the family. Cayce was a very friendly fellow, very affable and willing to talk about his work. Even then, at the very start, he did not seem like a stranger. I felt as if I'd always known him. He agreed to stay with us a week. And, of course, he gave us all readings. Everyone in the family.

I myself had the first reading, I think. I remember he told me of my own interest in psychic phenomena, and he told me then, too, that my future would be in uniform and that he saw me leaving the flock and fold and I would be gone for some time but I would return to the family.

In that first meeting in Lexington, he gave readings for our family and friends, talked about his work as a photographer, his dreams of success, and his psychic gifts, which he accepted but did not understand. Nor did he know why or how they had been given to him.

The psychic field was not an area we really knew anything about or in which we deeply believed at that time. It was like going to a fortuneteller and hearing him say things that seemed sometimes right and sometimes incredible or even preposterous.

Yet there was a unique excitement. He told us, for instance, how he had always been considered peculiar when around the other children. He told us also about the fact that very often he'd be playing with children that nobody saw but they were very real to him. He told us what the neighbors thought about him. He was always brought to parties and they'd ask him questions and he would answer but he thought very little about it . . . he thought about himself and the children. . . .

This was the beginning of the warm and wonderful relationship between the Cayces and the Kahns. It was a relationship that lasted a lifetime. It was to determine, form, and direct all my actions, all my effort, and whatever achievements I accomplished in my career in industry, in my service in two world wars, and civic and religious activities.

Cayce was really a young man at the time, despite the fact that he seemed pretty old from my teen-age perspective. And he was surely lonely—not everyone, indeed very few, on the outside understood the unique psychic gift he possessed. He needed people, apart from his own immediate family, who could understand and to whom he could pour out what the forces, these intuitions, this second world in which he lived, really meant.

I have always been sure that that was a part of the reason he took so readily to the Kahns. He was a member of the Christian Church, as his denomination was called, and we were a family of Reform Jews, a turbulent family of father and mother and nine youngsters and everybody busy with the things of the world, growing up, going to school, running a retail and wholesale grocery business in the midst of the horsy, bluegrass world of Lexington.

All of this played its part in his reaction to the seemingly accidental currents that brought him into the aura of our family. There was always a place for him in our home for as long as he needed or wanted to stay. He told us that we were his kin, that he was a part of us. He said, "I hope, Mother Kahn, you will take me into your family. . . ."

She did. So did we all.

At the time of my first meeting with Cayce I was still attending high school. My father, Solomon Kahn, came to America from Germany when he was sixteen, and went into the business of selling fine chinaware and kitchenware. In Cincinnati, Ohio, he met and married my mother and they moved to Lexington.

I was born in 1893, the year of the worst depression Kentucky had ever experienced, in fact the worst financial panic the country had known up until that time. Nobody, not even the wealthy race-horse owners of Lexington, had money to spend on expensive china. Moreover, the F. M. Kirby Company, forerunners of what was to be known as the five-and-ten cent store, had moved into Lexington and were selling a cup and saucer for ten cents where my father's imported cup and saucer cost two dollars.

This was when my mother told him that, in her opinion, fine chinaware was no business to be in in the midst of a depression. But people still had to eat, so she suggested that they go into the food business. He agreed that this was wise.

They opened a grocery store on the ground floor of a corner house, and we lived in a five-room apartment above it. I was about two years old when they moved to this location, at Fourth and Jefferson Streets. It was a neighborhood largely of Irish and Italian immigrants. There were virtually no other Jewish families. Growing up in such an area was a liberal education in cultural and religious traditions and beliefs.

By the time I was nine, however, my business career had begun. With pencil behind my ear and a loaf of bread in hand I would run across the street to deliver the bread to a blind customer.

One early incident relating to integrity in business occurred about this time. I happened to go into a bank in Lexington to get some forms. I heard a man say, "There comes his son now." Then one of the men told me the story I had not known. In the 1893 panic, my father had actually been forced into bankruptcy in his chinaware business. Almost at once, however, he began paying back those from whom he had purchased furniture and other supplies. The banker told me how he had explained to my father that under American law he was not obligated to pay debts of this kind after establishing bankruptcy.

But, he said, my father told him, "I didn't go into bankruptcy to get out of paying debts but only to give myself time so that I could pay."

In the seven years that followed, the banker revealed, my father had paid back every cent.

Fortunately, after that, my father became very successful in the grocery store operation, and expanded from time to time to additional stores. This led finally to our moving into Hampton Court. I remember it as a lovely house all of yellow brick with a large front porch. There was a library with a fireplace and a living room with large folding doors. The furniture was mahogany and the large dining room table was big enough for the whole family—including Mr. Cayce.

While we were all fond of Cayce from the start, my father did have certain reservations. This was because he had long religious training in Judaism and had never allowed any of us to forget our religious obligations. He himself was a Biblical scholar, a student of the Talmud, the Torah, and the Cabala. He could speak, read, and write Hebrew fluently. I remember my father reminding us of how Saul, when about to go into battle, called up the spirit of Samuel through the witch of Endor and Samuel demanded of Saul, "Why hast thou disquieted me, to bring me up?" And Samuel told him that he and his sons would die in the battle.

My father's attitude was that this was an instance in which

the dead were disturbed. He said he did not believe it was right to call up the dead.

Cayce explained that he was not calling up ghosts of the departed. "I do not deal with the dead or with spirits," he said. "Mine is more from my mind or from my unconscious mind, which I have no explanation for; I do not consult the dead."

My mother agreed that whatever it was, it was not spiritualism; it was something else, something we did not understand, but it was obviously not dealing in spirits. My father gradually became more interested and ultimately lent his entire support to what we were doing. Otherwise we would not have gone along with it.

All of this began while I was in high school. From there I went on to the University of Kentucky and had planned on a law career, which was interrupted by the war and my enlistment.

When Cayce first gave me a reading predicting that I would leave the flock and go into uniform, there was no immediate threat of war in sight in America, so I assumed he meant that I would become a policeman or a fireman. This I did not think very probable.

But we liked each other and kept in touch. Cayce agreed that he would give me readings whenever I asked. Any time I wrote him a letter or telephoned with a request for a reading, or sent him a request from anyone I knew, he would respond as quickly as he could. No one and nothing ever interfered with the friendship of Edgar Cayce and myself, or with Fannie Kahn, my mother, or with any member of my family

At Virginia Beach, where he eventually made his permanent home, there are records and carbon copies of letters in which he addressed my mother as Mother Kahn and there are her letters to him in which she discussed problems and, talking about her children, asked questions, and sought guidance about them or any friends who might need help.

They were the simple, homey letters of friends, of family. He would write that he was sorry he couldn't get to see her. He hadn't been well recently, "Suppose I've been trying to work when I shouldn't—really anxious to try to be of help —taxing myself when I should not. . . ." And Mother Kahn, writing about one of the girls for whom she had received a reading, "Being it [the pain] was around the heart, I thought it needed attention so I had to call the doctor. . . . He did not know what it was, but I did. I did all of the things you suggested in the readings and have her up and about, thank God. She is okay."

I knew that I could count on what Cayce told me. This was not superstition or hero worship; I felt that he was a guide; I accepted that without understanding exactly how I could be so sure. It was not health in my case that I was particularly concerned with; it was my future, my career, what I should do with my life. I sent him letters regularly and he would go into his hypnotic sleep and give a reading which his wife would take down, and they would mail it to me. To give an example:

We were still active in the grocery business in which we were supplying a number of large institutions with large quantities of all kinds of goods. One day, in response to a question as to how we might improve our business, Cayce sent back a startling suggestion. The schools and universities in central Kentucky, which had to feed 150 to 200 students a day, bought their canned goods in one-, two-, or three-pound cans. This meant a lot of cans had to be opened—in those days with an old-fashioned can opener. This was costly in time and effort. The reading said I should go to Chicago and get one-gallon cans of the same products. I had not heard of any such thing. But the information came from Cayce, and my parents believed we should follow this up at once. I went to Chicago, where I had never been before, and found the firm of the name given in the reading. I called on them, explained who I was, told them about our large grocery operation, and wound up not only buying the one-gallon cans but also making arrangements to become their representative in Lexington, Kentucky.

In a few weeks a full freight-car load of canned goods arrived. I had become the purveyor of fine foods to major institutions in the Lexington area. It was one of the first major business steps in which a Cayce reading gave me not only general guidance but the name, place, and means by which this guidance would be carried to successful realization.

I was a young man full of ambition, full of interest in the world around me in all its aspects. Cayce was my friend, whom I deeply respected. He represented a new avenue of spiritual life and development.

Because of the difference in age between Cayce and myself, and the vast respect in which I held him, I did not feel that I could call him by his first name. At the same time, "Mr. Cayce" seemed too formal and remote. I thought about it and finally lit upon the word "Judge" as one that held the concept of honor and respect. The word seemed to stand for the things he stood for, the depth of judgment and wisdom that he touched in the psychic world and also in his ordinary conscious life. I had the feeling that he would judge my life and my actions by the same high standards he held in his own. Almost from the start, and for the rest of our lives, I called him Judge.

CHAPTER 2

Judge

Later I would meet Cayce's wife and children and sisters and all his family. His mother was as tall as he was—tall and beautiful. She told me many stories about her son from the time he was two years old. She knew that he had this power. His father was very strict; a magistrate in the county where they lived, he believed in old-fashioned discipline.

Cayce's mother told me how once when he was around ten he came home from school with a note from the teacher saying that he had been inattentive in class. Edgar's father—whom Cayce in later years always called the "Squire"—went over his son's lessons with him that night and discovered that Edgar didn't know how to spell any of the words he was supposed to have learned. Edgar's mother told me she had to step in and stop her husband, who wanted to give the boy a sound whipping as one way of impressing upon him the importance of spelling.

Edgar had glanced at the spelling lesson—but other interests had interfered. Now he told his father, "Pa, let me go to sleep for five minutes on my book. Then I think I can go through with my spelling."

This statement, Mrs. Cayce told me, infuriated the Squire,

who had little patience with his son's peculiar notions, especially when they affected his education. But Cayce's mother convinced her husband to let his son go to sleep. It was only for five minutes, after all. Somewhat annoyed, the Squire said, "All right, then—go to sleep!"

"He woke up in about five minutes"—here I'm quoting Mother Cayce—"and handed his father the book and was able to spell the words in the book from cover to cover and could tell on what page the word was printed."

However, the book that came to interest him most was not a spelling book but the Bible. Although Cayce's formal education ended with the sixth grade, this book he read, once each year throughout his life, from cover to cover. He became a teacher in Sunday school, and preached in the Campbellite Christian Church until he went to Virginia Beach, where he became a member of the Presbyterian Church. Hugh Lynn Cayce, Judge's older son, later became a deacon and then an elder in the Presbyterian Church.

Cayce's father took very seriously his role as family head and community leader. Everyone respected him. The family was and is prominent in Hopkinsville. The name Cayce is a good solid name in that section of the country—Bowling Green, Hopkinsville, Kentucky, and Selma, Alabama. Judge insisted that he would never willingly do anything to demean that name. His gift was not designed for carnival routines.

For the skeptics and scoffers, this background out of which Cayce emerged is important. It was one of respectability, propriety, morality, and in large measure, normalcy.

He was capable of profound concepts and intimations in his conscious life as well as in hypnotic trance. Sometimes he would quote from his own readings, adding his conscious interpretations of things he had said in the unconscious. "Life in its essence," he wrote to me once, quoting liberally from the readings, "is a manifestation of the divine intelligence or force we call God. . . . So, all healing must come from God, through this essence of manifestation of God in the physical body. Whether the intelligence that brings such a healing consciousness is from a drug, a mechanical appliance, an operation, or the very foods we eat or what not, it is in essence from one and the same source. The readings then are merely a channel through which such information may come as to assist one in understanding what would produce coordination in the individual body. That is saying it must come from a universal source, if it is to be trustworthy. If it does not come from the cosmic, or universal, or God source, it is just as apt to be detrimental as it is to be constructive.

"So, let us hope this work [his work] is a manifestation of the universal force or source. I believe it to be. . . .

"This may or may not be a real explanation of the work. It may sound to some as if we are claiming some connection or association with God that is superior or above others, but this is far from true; for the work has ever followed—and is following—this first and most basic truth: 'Know, O Israel, the Lord thy God is One!'"

It was clear in this letter that Cayce himself was developing a greater articulation—as if he were learning from the readings too, the conscious Cayce learning from the unconscious self.

Surely, no man who could write, speak, think in such terms as these could have any element of fraud or fakery in his being.

This I knew beyond any doubt—young and untutored as I may have been at that time.

When I first met Cayce, we were very young, our world was young, and Kentucky in those days was certainly not all somber and serious. Anything but, in fact. It was a colorful, exciting world. Fayette County, where I was born, is bluegrass country, made famous by horse breeders and fanciers who came down there from New York to buy those beautiful stock farms—people like the Harkness family and the Harry Payne Whitneys. The Phoenix Hotel in Lexington was a headquarters for all the great horsemen and when they were in town, in October, it was truly an assemblage of some of the most prominent people in the nation.

I remember a boisterous occasion when one of the young millionaires brought down a double-decker bus with six horses. He also had thirty girls. And a fellow sitting up on top with a bugle. They went right through the middle of Lexington, with people on the streets cheering them on.

Most of the horse people were delightful. One I came to know was David Look, head of The Corn Exchange Bank, who had bought a stock farm in Lexington. I recall meeting him one day at the Phoenix Hotel. I was brash and not afraid of speaking up to a man and I told him about our store and said we would appreciate very much having his patronage. He said he would give me a sixty-day trial and if we made good he would give us his business. I was to get in touch with his general manager.

I drove out and saw the general manager and the result was that we sold and delivered large shipments of food to this stock farm for years. We called our place the Food Emporium. Customers used to drive up with their horse and wagons and push our service buttons with their buggy whips and I would give them instant service. Through Mr. Look we made contacts with all the stock farm people. When Edgar Cayce came to town he met many of them. In those days people looked askance at Edgar. Mother always talked about Cayce; she never let up about Cayce's work and what it could mean.

Our family had three stores then, three stores that sold everything farmers could use. But for the farmers themselves it was hard going. The tobacco companies made money but the farmers who grew the tobacco had a fight just to stay alive.

The row was long and hard. They would burn the ground, then plant the seeds, in February or March, and cover them with a thin gauze cloth to keep the sun from getting too close to them and to keep the bugs away. When the plants were two inches tall they would take them from under the gauze and transplant them, about two feet apart, in the dark Fayette County soil.

Then the plants would grow until they reached five to six feet tall and the leaves were a foot and a half to two feet long. And the bugs would attack them and the farmer had to spray them with Paris green in those days and would clip small pieces out of the top so that the plant would spread. When the plants were fully grown, huge bugs called suckers would try to destroy them and the farmer and his children would have to go along and pull off these suckers and kill them.

I came to know all this because my father would finance the farmers from the time they put the seed into the ground. He furnished them with everything they needed. We had a downtown store and a country store at the edge of the city where the farms were. When they sold the tobacco the owner of the land—which was not usually the farmer—got half of the take. This was only six cents a pound at that time. Prices were so low they really broke the back of almost every farm family in the community.

Then some of the men banded together to try to get better prices for the farmers. One such group, called night riders, dressed in black and rode on horses at night to keep most of the farmers from selling tobacco to the big companies that year. Later, official union people came in and did get better prices for the farmers finally.

The company would buy at auctions in the warehouse. I would go to the pay table at the auction and take out what was owed to us, but if there wasn't enough money for the farmer, my father always would carry the debt for another year. My father died in 1918, and there was a great deal of money owed to him that we never collected. The farmer never could catch up.

Cayce was involved in this, too. His father was a farmer, and Judge himself knew farming since the Cayce family grew the burley tobaccos used in cigarettes and pipe mixtures. As a result, he gave readings for a lot of farmers in the area. Of course, in those days he did not keep records, but I can tell you from memory that many of these farmers were helped or cured by means of the readings Cayce gave. My mother had gotten a reading from Cayce for a farmer in which Fenner's Golden Relief was prescribed. Fenners, a liniment made in Buffalo, New York, was used by people with arthritis. It was little known then until it came through the reading. However, after the first reading, we began to sell it in the grocery store and continued to stock it for years. Then along came Sloan's Liniment, and to this day nothing takes its place in soothing aches and pains.

There had been in one of Cayce's early readings about himself the statement that there would come a Jew into his life who would work closely with him and help to shape his future.

Judge himself told me of this, and it was clear he thought I was the one who would fulfill this prophecy from the reading. The pattern of our family and our lives more than supported this view.

We were a Jewish family, a deeply religious Jewish family, growing up in an area on the edge of the rock-ribbed Southern Bible belt. Both my parents believed in living their faith. At the time of my birth my father was president of the Orthodox Jewish temple in Lexington. The Reform movement, to which we later belonged, came in later. There were only ten Jewish families in the city—all of them Orthodox. We brought in a rabbi from Cincinnati who had curls and wore a long coat and was typical of what you might see in Palestine and Eastern Europe.

Eventually there were forty or fifty Jewish families in Lexington and one day my father announced that he wanted to start a Reform congregation in Lexington. He did launch a Reform group that held meetings in the Odd Fellows Hall until they were able to buy a Lutheran church and turn it into a Reform temple. This was a very liberal temple. I taught Sunday school there—on Sunday morning.

There were many gay times in Lexington for young people growing up. I was working in the store, earning most of my expenses; my friendship with Cayce was deepening. I went to many of the local parties and dances, had many girl friends. One of the young ladies I danced with, Mona, was a true Kentucky beauty who ultimately became known to the world as Mrs. Harrison Williams. Long afterward, people would point out her home in Paris, Kentucky, and say, "Her husband left her a hundred million dollars." And I would say, "Yes, but when I knew her, her father was a horse trainer. . . ."

Judge would come to some of the dances but he would never dance himself. Sometimes we drove to Frankfort, twenty-six miles away. They held dances there on a riverboat, and would bring in bands from various parts of the country. But one night my mother showed some of her own psychic force—she told me not to go to the dance at the Frankfort riverboat that night.

She had very strong feelings about it so I agreed not to go. But the seat I was to occupy was taken—although I did not know it at the time—by one of my closest friends. On the way to Frankfort there was an accident. The boy in the seat I was to have occupied was killed.

It was a pattern of all youth—striving, struggling young people growing up, reaching into maturity. Kentucky for me was a world of work and play; it was the business of achieving and getting ahead. It was also bourbon country. Among some in the younger set there was considerable drinking even then. Kentucky made the best bourbon whisky in the world, especially in Bourbon County, eighteen miles from Lexington. According to the legends and stories, there were three causal elements involved in Kentucky bourbon supremacy—limestone water, the mellow climate, and the rich soil which is fed by the limestone water and which produces both Kentucky's famous bluegrass and also the corn used in the production of Kentucky bourbon. These in turn, it is claimed, are responsible for three other developments: The fact that the most beautiful women in the world come from Kentucky; the fact that Kentucky horses have narrow legs, which make them famous as racers and trotters; and the fact that Lexington and Louisville became bourbon centers of the world. Such are the claims, for none of which I could personally vouch.

Cayce would take an occasional drink like anyone else—but I never saw him drunk. He smoked, but I never saw him smoke to excess. He tasted life like any other young man but never overdid it. He lived as any normal human being did—except when he was in that special hypnotic sleep, which he put himself into and in which he gave readings without knowing where the information came from or having any idea after he awakened what he had said.

Judge told me of one instance which occurred early in his career, before I met him. While he was asleep, the questioner asked something about a horse race and who would win. Cayce, without hesitation, gave the man the name of the winner. This brought the man a windfall of thousands of dollars, and he disappeared almost immediately with his winnings. Two years later this man wrote Cayce from a mental institution in New Orleans, begging Cayce for a reading on how to get out.

Cayce did give this man a reading and guidance which enabled him to obtain official release. But Judge swore from that moment on never to take any other cases involving race horses or gambling of any type.

I now began to realize that Cayce's prediction that I would go into uniform perhaps had meant not a uniform of some local public service, but of the United States Army. That we would be involved in the world conflagration which had erupted in 1914 was becoming clear beyond all doubt, in my opinion. My parents had come from Germany and felt deeply the debt they owed this country. I decided to join in the efforts to prepare America for war.

Through friends I obtained an introduction to our senator in Washington and through him received what amounted to an "honorary" commission of a second lieutenancy in the Army, early in 1917. By the beginning of April, I was in New York City, recruiting in front of the New York Public Library at Forty-second Street and Fifth Avenue. In the course of this work for the Army I had the honor of meeting and introducing to the crowds many of the world-famed figures who came to this country during that time, among them French General Foch, Marshal Joffre, Lord Balfour, and other world dignitaries of that day.

To do this job I had to talk a great deal out of doors, against the chill winds and the roar of Fifth Avenue traffic. One night I found that I had all but lost my voice. Often I would sit in the lobby of the Hotel Girard in the evening talking with friends and people I had met. Mostly I talked to them about my great interest in Edgar Cayce, and his ability to help others. The friends were interested but skeptical. On that particular evening, partly to prove my point but mainly to get help, I told them that I would give them a demonstration. I would send a telegram which they would see in advance asking Cayce to give me certain information. As always, in accordance with his instructions and invariable method, I would tell him nothing. Before sending this telegram I showed it to some of those who were gathered there in the lobby.

This message—although the actual transmitted wording may have varied in some minor word—stated in essence: *Please tell me why I am in New York. Advise as to my physical condition and what I should do next. David E. Kahn.*

Because of the war situation involving the United States, all honorary commissions such as mine had been canceled. The wording of Cayce's reply to my message, again essentially as received, read as follows:

"You are in New York in regard to final commission in U. S. Army. Pull will get you nothing. Apply to army post nearest you in New York as training camps will open May 15. You will be accepted. As to physical condition you have lost voice by exposure to weather. This is prescription: cherry bark from north side of cherry tree, taken three times a day."

I obtained the cherry bark and took it to a druggist who prepared it for me. The condition might have gotten better, whether I used the preparation or not. In any case, within three days after I took the cherry bark the throat condition was cleared up.

More important to many of those who had seen the original telegram was the fact that my friend Judge had diagnosed my condition with no indications from a distance of hundreds of miles.

I followed the rest of Cayce's instructions promptly.

On Sunday morning, I went to Governors Island in the New York harbor, the main army post in the area, and talked with the commanding officer. I told him that I had been instructed to come to see him about a commission in the Army, and that this was in connection with the army training camp that was to open on May 15.

The commanding officer, a huge, handsome, old-line army

man, flushed with sudden anger. He demanded to know where I had obtained information regarding the opening of these officer-training camps, particularly since I named the exact date.

"Nobody knows about this yet," he declared. "The information has not been released to the public."

In a more security-minded age, I might have spent the next few days undergoing interrogations and possible arrest. Moreover, I could hardly tell the commanding officer the real truth without very probably compromising myself as possible army officer material.

I told him I learned this from other army personnel with whom I had been associated while recruiting in New York and the answer apparently satisfied him.

But he kept on, nevertheless, asking about my background, my honorary second lieutenant's commission, my work in recruiting in New York. Finally he agreed to accept me as the very first candidate for officer's training in the new training-camp program about to go into operation.

I was first to have been sent to Camp Plattsburgh in New York but I learned that Fort Benjamin Harrison in Indianapolis, Indiana, was also to be opened for officers training. I asked and was given permission to go to this training camp, which was much closer than Plattsburgh to my home.

The commanding officer at Governors Island, however, couldn't give me any transfer papers for this shift to Fort Harrison. When I reached there, I explained the situation to the officer in charge. I was in uniform, I said, because I had been recruiting in New York City. I had not had time to get papers from the camp in New York.

Within an hour, the enlistment officer had cleared up the situation to his satisfaction and announced that I was accepted at Fort Harrison as an officer candidate. As I recall, that was May 15, 1917. Three months later I was to be commissioned as a second lieutenant in the United States Army. This time it would be no honorary title they could take away.

This was the first fulfillment of the prophecy I had from Cayce. During the training period, I continued to have readings and guidance from Judge. He told me I would do well at this camp and would get ahead swiftly. The readings and the messages he sent to me told me how to conduct myself. They said that I was to think about assisting in the management of the camp and that I was to get into the area of looking after the welfare of the soldiers.

I had been there only about twenty-four hours when this part of the role Cayce had suggested in the readings began to take shape.

An order came down that no leave would be granted for some weeks. There were thousands of other young men like myself in training to become officers. It looked like we were in for an extremely difficult time.

The readings had said that I was to serve the needs of the troops—the men and officers of the American Army. I decided the first opportunity had arrived. I would try to find some means, within the limits of army and camp regulations, to provide entertainment and release from tension for the thousands of army personnel pent up in the cramped military confines.

CHAPTER 3

"You Will Go with Honor..."

Dice and card games were permitted in the camp but no visitors were allowed and no leaves. Knowing that these men were in for a rough time, knowing also that the readings indicated I would have to do something "unusual" during this period of my military career I decided that most of all the men in training here needed some kind of entertainment. On my own initiative, I dropped in on several regimental headquarters and asked that anyone who could play an instrument or sing a song give me his name and the address of his company. I told them we were going to put on a show, an impromptu show, Friday night at eight o'clock.

No one had told me—or ordered me—to put on a show—or even suggested that it might be a good idea.

I was doing this on my own, on the hunch that there had to be some solid talent in a camp crowded with men from all over the country. The hunch paid off. I found we had a number of people with show business backgrounds—musicians, young actors, singers, soft shoe dancers, comedians. My own stage experience was limited to participation—somewhat successfully—in amateur high school plays and musicals. I told all the army theatrical recruits to meet me later in front of the Post Exchange to work out details and times for trying out individual acts. They were glad to do it. I knew there would be little or no time for real rehearsals.

Next, I called on the wife of the commanding general of the fort and asked her if she would like to have reservations for the show we were going to put on Friday night. All seats were free, of course. The general's wife reserved places for herself, the general, their daughter, and the general's aide, a good-looking young lieutenant.

From there I went next door to speak with the wife of the chief of staff. I explained that the general's wife had made four reservations for the show we were putting on Friday night; How many would she and the chief of staff require? Within a very short time I had more than two hundred reservations.

Now I had an audience and a cast—all I needed was a theater, stage, lights, seats for people to sit on. I went over to the office of the quartermaster.

I said, "Colonel, you know that we are putting on a show?"

The colonel said, "Why, yes. My wife made some reservations for seats."

I explained to him that this thing had sprung up spontaneously but I told him also what I needed: A temporary stage that could be made by laying a platform on top of wooden horses. And I wanted two hundred chairs for the officers and wives and one thousand watt lamps.

On Friday night everything was ready. By six-thirty the formations began to move in on the improvised theater and some thousand men were seated on the ground waiting for the performance.

I went up on the platform and greeted the general and his wife and this tremendous throng of men. I told them that this show was not rehearsed and that I had no idea what was going to come forward. I said, "You can tell us if you like it by your applause and maybe we will continue it in some form in the weekends to follow."

The show began with two Kentuckians, one six foot four inches, the other barely five feet tall. Both came from feuding families in the Kentucky mountains. They had become friends in the service even though their kinfolk greeted each other with shotguns.

The two staged a blank-cartridge Kentucky mountain farce about feuds that had the audience roaring and set the tempo of a performance that clearly was what this audience of pent-up troops in training for battle wanted. Admittedly, it was not too hard to please them. But the impromptu production had a rousing reception.

The following morning I had a call from the colonel in charge of the area where I had taken up quarters. He wanted to know, among other things, how I happened to have given that show the previous night.

I said, "Did I do anything against regulations?"

"It isn't a question of doing anything wrong," he said. "The question is who gave you the authority to do it?"

I explained again, in great detail, how it was just something that sprang up because of need and circumstances. I did not dare tell him how I had instructions, through a trance reading from Judge, that I was to play a part in helping to build the morale of the men in this camp.

My plan had worked out thus far, but at that point the colonel said abruptly, "General Glenn wants to see you at once."

I asked him if I was in trouble and he said, "You'll hear from the general." I said, "Well, Colonel, you know, I'm no real army man." He said, "Well, when you go in, you come up here to the general and you put your heels together like this and salute him and say, 'Sir, Private Kahn reporting from the 13th Company.'" Then he said, "When he gets through with the conversation, you salute him again and you put your toe back and you turn and get out."

I was not actually worried. The readings had said also that so long as I did what I knew was right, I would not get into trouble with superior officers.

The first question the general asked was about my background. I told him I was raised in the grocery business. Had I had any theatrical experience? I told him no. He said, "Kahn, what gave you the idea to put on a show like this last night?"

"It was just something to keep us all busy," I said. "Something to help us until we were allowed to visit Indianapolis on weekends."

"Could you put on a show like this every week?"

I said we could do it but not in the same impromptu way. I told him what we would have to have—a regular stage, lights, curtains, wiring, seats. It would cost about five hundred dollars. I said I thought the movie makers would let us have first-run motion pictures as part of the war effort.

General Glenn told me that he considered this whole thing an amazing performance. He said, "I want you to become the director of amusements."

I was to have a car with a chauffeur. The general wanted a new show every weekend. He picked up the telephone, called the manager of the Post Exchange and ordered him to report at once. When the manager arrived, General Glenn told him to put aside whatever I needed to finance the performances I was to put on at Fort Benjamin Harrison.

The Post Exchange manager, a major, said, "Yes, sir."

We both saluted the general, turned smartly, and went out.

From then on, anything I needed for the performances was available through the major. On official duty, although still a private, I had my chauffeur-driven car take me into Indianapolis and I worked out an arrangement with the manager of the Keith Vaudeville Theater whereby they would send us one act a week as the highlight of our regular weekly shows. All I had to promise was that we would send our car to pick up the performers and bring them back. It was only fifteen miles from the camp.

To the best of my knowledge, that was the real beginning of programed entertainment for American troops in the camps by professional performers of the American theater.

Every week or so during this period, I either got a letter from Judge or I wrote him. Often he would respond with a reading. The answers and suggestions in the readings made it possible for me to move without any fear that I would step out of line with the military, with whom I had had little previous experience.

Each of the readings would tell me how to arrange different plans involved. For instance, I had one reading regarding the timing as to when I should ask four governors of nearby states to come as our guests. The reading said we should invite them all at the same time. I therefore wrote to the four governors as well as to Secretary of War Newton Baker, inviting them all to attend our performance at the camp. As I was the camp's director of amusements, I did not have to get the permission of the general to send invitations; I merely signed them as "by direction of Major General Edwin F. Glenn."

The four governors were from Kentucky, Ohio, West Virginia, and Indiana. They all accepted. I also asked the Secretary of War to review the troops. On the eventful day, I stood with the four governors, the generals and colonels, and all the general staff to review the training camp at Fort Harrison. In the files of the Indianapolis *News* you can still find the headlines on the inner pages: "Sergeant Kahn announces program for this week. . . ."

Things happen. Sometimes you make them happen and sometimes you let them happen, let them, in a psychic sense, unfold. Largely in the way and in the direction indicated in the readings I had from Cayce, I simply allowed things to unfold.

I was sent to Camp Taylor at Louisville, Kentucky, and from there to the officers' staff at Fort Worth, Texas, where I trained with the 36th Division. We were training in preparation for going overseas. My bunkmate in the camp, a legislator from Bourbon County, was one of the first to be sent across. He was killed in his first month of action in France.

I was in constant touch with Cayce. And, naturally, I talked about him. Many people asked for more details. I would tell them what I knew. Many would ask me if I could get them readings. One request in Texas came from a woman who had been leading a fast life in a Northern city and was now under hospital care, suffering from a lung ailment. I telephoned Cayce and he agreed to come out—for enough to cover his expenses and time. As a result of his reading for this girl, she broke up her relationship with her sweetheart. Eventually she met a man whom she truly loved. Long afterward, I ran into her in another city. She said to me, "Mr. Kahn, you are the only one who knows anything about my background and what happened. I am now married and a mother and we are so very happy. . . ."

I assured her that I had no idea what she was talking about and what the incident was. It had completely gone out of my memory.

When Cayce came out for that reading, he remained several weeks, staying at the Fort Worth Country Club. Through various associations, including the Masons, which I joined at that time, I had come to know many of the young people in town and many of the fine families and leaders in the city. During this three-week period many people heard about and wanted to meet—or have readings from—this man. The story spread. He became a celebrity during his stay in Fort Worth. All kinds of people sought him—army personnel, the wealthy of the city, the young set and the old, as well as average people needing help. Many of the readings were medical. There were those who denounced him. There were also those who called him "some kind of saint."

At this period, I was serving under Major General E. St. John Greble, also known as E. St. John the Devil because he was a strict enforcer of army regulations. I happened to be officer of the day when he arrived and I not only arranged transportation but also had a good fire going in the pot-bellied stove because a norther had blown up that night. I also had on his table a quart bottle of bourbon I'd brought from Kentucky. Later, I became his permanent aide.

Not too long after E. St. John the Devil arrived, word came through that the division would be leaving by the following Friday for "parts unknown"—which usually meant front lines in France. At the same time one of my younger brothers, Leon, died. Leon had been injured in a fall from a wagon at the age of two and had suffered from convulsions. Judge gave him readings and suggested treatments but the doctors refused to carry them out as he suggested. They thought the prescriptions were dangerous. Cayce told me he was certain Leon would have survived if the doctors had done what the readings said. They didn't. Whether following the Cayce readings would have saved him became a moot question. Leon was dead.

I wanted leave to be with my family for a few days; for this reason I had to know what was going to happen to this division and to my chance of being able to get home to help my mother and my family.

Out on the parade grounds was a pay telephone, and I put through a call from there to Selma, Alabama, where Cayce had moved. When I reached Cayce I said, "Judge, I have two questions, please listen to me very intently. I want to know if I will be able to get a leave of absence to go home to my family and if I can stay two or three weeks when I get there. If I cannot go I want to know why. I'd like to know what is going to happen to me in the next six weeks."

As in all Cayce readings, I gave him no further information. I said I would wait by the phone for him to call back and reverse the charges. I knew he understood how very urgent it was to me.

Some time later, the phone rang. It was Judge. "You can go home for three weeks if you want," he told me, "because you are not leaving Texas when you think. There'll be an order very soon directing troops now on the Mexican border to report to your divison to be inducted into the national Army.

"The commanding general is not going with the division when you go, but you will not go for at least three months. When you get the notice to go, the general is going to give you the opportunity to go with him to Virginia as his aide, or to go with the division under a new general. You will go with the division."

The reading amplified this advice with the words: "You will go with honor, and you'll come with honor; you'll have many narrow escapes but you'll never have an accident. You will come back in good health. You will see you will move with the division and you will be successful."

The following morning, after breakfast, I was alone with General Greble. I told him I would like to make a prophecy. I told him that we would not be leaving at the end of the week. I said we would not leave for at least three months. I said further that I thought we would have a lot of soldiers brought up from the border who would be inducted from the National Guard into the regular Army and that we would train them for overseas duty.

"But when we do go overseas, sir," I told him, "you are not going with the division. I think you are going to have a continued training program to carry out. . . ."

After listening to me, the general said with no sign of emotion, "Where did you get this information?"

I said that I couldn't tell him at the moment, but that I would tell him if he asked me about it at a later time.

He then showed me some orders received from Washington, stamped with the seal of the adjutant general and countersigned by Secretary of War Newton Baker. These were the official orders sending our division abroad. The general informed me that this effectively ruled out any of the predictions I had just been making.

I was not sure whether he knew about Cayce's visit to Fort Worth or about the readings I had from him. In any event, I told him, "Very well, sir. But we have an understanding. If you want to know the full facts, I'll tell you."

Twenty-four hours later, a West Point major who was also one of the general's aides, came into my tent, which was next to the general's, and told me, "General Greble wants me to tell you that the orders have just come through to detrain, that you understand why he is telling you this, and that he will see you later."

The general did not mention the matter when I saw him. Three months afterward, shortly before the division did leave for Europe, General Greble sent for me and demanded, "Kahn, who the hell told you I wasn't going with the division?"

That was when I told him the whole story, including the story of my phone call to Cayce in Selma and what Cayce reported in the reading when he called me back.

He listened in silence. Then he said, "These are my orders today. I am retired but I am to go to Virginia, where I am to train the new recruits."

I said, "Sir, may I tell you why you sent for me? It is because you are going to offer me the opportunity either to go with you as your aide or to go overseas with the division. Cayce also told me that."

There was a warmth of friendship between us and I felt it in that moment as he stood there, looking at me, the telegram from Washington in his hand.

Very gently, he asked, "What did he say you should do?"

I said, "He told me that I would go with honor and come with honor and that I would have many narrow escapes but never an accident and that I should go."

And General Greble said, "If I were as young as you and I had to swim the Atlantic to get there, I'd go too. But now I'm retired and I'm going to train troops. You go."

When I did go overseas it was with another general who took over the division and who I believe later went to West Point as commandant.

I never saw General Greble again but we remained friends and corresponded and I had some letters from him while I was in France. Later I learned that he lost his sight and some time after that I heard he had died at Walter Reed Hospital in Washington.

These are the facts relative to Judge and one of his most extraordinary prophecies. I learned eventually that some of my mail had been intercepted. Cayce also told me that he had been notified by Washington that they wanted an interview with him to discuss some of the work he was doing and the correspondence he was having with some of the officers in the Army. Someone, apparently, had alerted them to this man and his powers. Whether this was their first hint that there could be a power of perception beyond the usual avenues of communication I never was able to verify.

So far as I know, however, no official interviews between Edgar Cayce and any of the intelligence people in the War Department ever took place.

One can only speculate on what results such a confrontation might have produced.

BOOK TWO

Guides

"Be consistent in all thou doest, and when thou hast conquered self thou mayest be able to govern another. He who approaches for mercy, grace, and counsel may not have sought against his brother, but must be able to appreciate and understand that he already has in hand. . . ."

Fragment of one of Edgar Cayce's readings
for his friend, David E. Kahn
May 4, 1937

CHAPTER 4

Four Hundred Pairs of Shoes

I accepted as an indisputable fact Judge's assurance that I would come through every danger in the war unscathed. Holding approximately the same post in France that I had in the States—as a general's aide—I went everywhere, to the front, into the trenches, over open and unprotected areas, often under shelling or bombing. I simply was not afraid; Cayce had said I would be all right.

The dangers Cayce predicted I would encounter were present almost from our first day out on the S.S. *George Washington,* converted from ocean liner to transport. This was the vessel Woodrow Wilson used when he went abroad to fight for the League of Nations. It was a hazardous crossing; we were under attack a number of times from enemy submarines. Fortunately we lost none of our ships in the convoy. But we had one tragic loss on board our ship.

A young soldier quartered on lower deck—a youth from Oklahoma—committed suicide by shooting himself. He left a note stating that his reason for this act was that he was "skeered."

A curious epilogue occurred many years later, when I had

all but forgotten the suicide. I participated in a seance in Dallas, Texas, and the boy appeared and gave me the details, through the medium, of why he killed himself. He assured me that there was continuity of life; he said it was shown by the fact that he could come back to me now through this eighty-five-year-old woman, in a fully lighted room. Present at that time was Edgar Cayce, as well as a lieutenant who had served with me in France.

I considered this experience extremely significant. While Cayce himself was not active in spiritualism, we did probe wherever we could into matters that touched on the metaphysical or the psychic world. For me, this particular incident in the seance helped to confirm—years after the episode—my own long-held opinion and belief that there is no death, not as many think it to be. There is continuity of the soul.

When we landed in Brest we trudged over muddy roads out to our encampment area. I found myself back at my old assignments, billeting, locating quarters for division headquarters and for the general, setting up the Post Exchange. We were in the environs of a place called Bar-sur-Aube. It was in midsummer; fields and farms and vineyards were in full bloom all around us. I had the rank of captain; assisting me was a young lieutenant, Lorenzo Kilmer, Jr., who was to be my friend for many years.

The Post Exchange we set up was a financial success and with the profits we bought foodstuffs and candy to pass out to the children when we went on inspection trips. During this stage of my journey, I met many wonderful persons who were to be part of my life and career in later years. One of them I recall was the chief quartermaster of the Army, General Robert Wood, later to become head of Sears, Roebuck—a firm with whom I was to do considerable business.

I had continued to be in touch with Cayce by letter. He

continued to tell me no harm could or would come to me. Also, in one reading regarding my career both in the Army and afterward, Cayce said my opportunities were "many and various" in business, and added, "and of the financial wonderful."

That was in a reading of March 7, 1918. He told me that in performance of army duties, I was to listen to "dictates of heart and conscience and make no resistance to the living guide," by which the reading indicated he meant the voice speaking within myself.

Later, an incident occurred close to the front lines. The trenches were just ahead of us; contingents of our division were moving into action as called for. I received an order—at night—to attain and bring up immediately to this area four hundred pairs of desperately needed shoes for one contingent scheduled to go into action in four hours.

It was night and raining and the mud was up to your neck. To get across it could be worth your life.

I told the officer who gave me this order that of course I would do it, but that he had to understand that I had no experience in this kind of thing. His laconic answer was, "Well, you'll have it by the time you get back."

So I started out in the car to get four hundred pairs of shoes. Sheets of rain swept across the windshield. I reached the quartermaster's depot safely, got out and pounded on the door of the colonel in charge. The colonel opened the door finally, made a few blasphemous comments, and demanded to know by whose order I dared to wake him up in the middle of the night. I told him, "Sir, by order of Major General William Smith. I have a message for you personally."

The colonel opened the door wider and said, "Come in."

I told him about the desperately needed shoes. "They'll trade the shoes they have on now for the shoes you've got at the Post. They've got to have them."

He wanted to see a written order for these shoes.

I said I hadn't had time to get a written order. "I was asked to get these shoes because the men are moving in a matter of hours."

The colonel called a sergeant and they let me have the four hundred pairs of shoes. I piled them into the car and drove back through the storm to headquarters. Two days later, I was called into General Smith's office. He wanted to know since when I was issuing orders in his name.

"It was the only way we could get the shoes, General," I said. "And we had to have them."

I told him the colonel I woke up was mean enough and angry enough to have me in the brig if I had told him somebody less than the general sent me. I said, "But our men went into action with good shoes on their feet."

General Smith seemed mollified. He thought about it a moment and said, "What else have you done in my name?"

I told him that on the way to various places I had seen trucks strewn around unused or abandoned, and guns lying all over the battlefield and I had issued an order in his name that men returning for periods of rest from the trenches should bring in the guns they could pick up and stack them at the railhead. All of these arms were government property and a lot could be reused. All this material was salvaged—in his name.

General Smith didn't seem too outraged. In fact, that was the origin of the Salvage Division of the 36th Division and General Smith made me Division Salvage Officer. We saved all kinds of material and conserved American property, blankets, guns, and ammunition.

Whatever I did and whatever role I played developed directly out of my unswerving confidence in the Cayce readings. The readings said that whenever I saw something that needed to be done, I should do it, acting on my own but in accordance with guidance of heart and conscience. Daring to act—daring also always to go directly to the top—became two rules of my life.

An example, involving Paris and the Jewish High Holidays, arose about two months after our division reached France. A Texas army captain from the 141st Infantry came up to Division Headquarters one day in early fall. He told me there were two hundred and fifty Jewish troops in the division in his location and that these men like everybody else had the right to observe their religious holidays. The Jewish New Year came early in September that year. His plan had been to send them up to Paris, which had the only synagogue they knew of. But the captain had received an order countermanding this proposal; a previous order still in effect forbade any troops going to Paris unless they had been in the area at least four months.

So the captain came to me. I said I would do something about it right away. I went to the division chief of staff, a colonel. He was annoyed. "Kahn," he said, "I think I'm just as good a Christian as you are a Jew and if this were Christmas I certainly wouldn't ask for any such privilege. We may go into action any day."

I said I could understand his feelings but that maybe the Jews ought to get a little more consideration because we were so many thousands of years older than Christianity and didn't he think age should have some credit? He smiled at this half humorous question and then said, "Well, why don't you go in and talk it over with General Smith?"

I went in and told General Smith we had a problem of Jewish soldiers not being able to celebrate the High Holidays. General Smith said, "Oh, you mean Rosh Hashanah and Yom Kippur?"

The way he said it, I thought for a moment he was Jewish himself, but he said no, he wasn't, but for many years he had made it a practice to attend religious services of all faiths, wherever he was on duty in the Army. He was sorry that the order for the men to go to Paris had been countermanded.

I suggested that if the matter were brought to General Pershing's attention, he might make a special ruling in this case. "Going back to the history of our people," I said, "even in the days of King David and King Solomon, when they were ready to go to war, they allowed their men to go before the Ark which contained the Torah with the Laws of Moses and on their knees they would pledge allegiance to the protection of their country. It seems to me no different today; here in a strange country, these men should be allowed to go to the nearest synagogue and there, as in those ancient days, pledge their allegiance to the welfare of our great country."

General Smith said, "I believe you are right. This matter should be brought to the attention of our General Headquarters." He called in the sergeant and told him he wanted to get in touch with General Pershing.

The call went through and the facts were presented tersely to the general-in-chief of America's expeditionary forces in France. All I heard was, "Yes, sir. . . . No, sir. . . . Thank you, sir. . . ." He hung up and turned back to me. "General Pershing directs you to proceed to Paris for three days with your men with rations and pay allowances and they should be billeted for those three days, going and coming, and they should also return for the Yom Kippur holiday, which would be eight or nine days later. . . ."

At my suggestion the Texas captain who was a line officer, and who had first brought the matter to my attention, was placed in command of the two hundred and fifty men. I went along as the divisional general's representative to see that everything was in order and that our men made a good impression on their first visit to Paris.

We arrived around five o'clock in the afternoon on the Rue de la Victoire in Paris where the synagogue was located. We had no time to send previous notice of our arrival. One can imagine the consternation of the hundreds of people crowded into the synagogue on the High Holiday when they looked up and saw two hundred and fifty men in uniform seeking to join in the services.

The scene was like something out of an opera. The man who came to greet us at the door was dressed like Napoleon. He had a cockadoodle hat, knee-buckled trousers, and the tri-colour of France across his chest with all his decorations. He was very pleased at this unique "invasion" and delighted that an aide of the general of the United States 36th Division was also present. He treated the men, the captain, and myself with the greatest consideration.

He went forward and spoke to a gentleman at the front of the temple. In high hat and Prince Albert coat, this gentleman immediately came up the aisle to welcome us. He was Baron Edward de Rothschild, president of the synagogue. The baron greeted us graciously, welcomed the men, and they were given whatever seats were vacant or could be set up in the aisles. I was taken to the pew of Baron Rothschild. During the course of the meeting, the baron asked me if I could read Hebrew. I said yes, I had been trained as a child and that although I could not recall much Hebrew scripture by heart I could read it. The baron then said, "I would like to have you go up to the Ark and parade with the Torahs, as is the custom in our temple."

The Torahs are on a parchment and contain the five books of Moses. It is a custom among the Orthodox to hand a guest one of those Torahs to parade around the temple, down one aisle and up another. I followed the baron in this ritualistic role.

As we passed by, the worshipers paid homage to the Torahs

by kissing shawls they wore around their shoulders and pressing the shawls to the scrolls. When we came back to the platform, which was occupied by the chief rabbi of France, the Torahs were opened and the chapters for those days were read. I recited the prayer before they opened the scroll, and after the reading, recited the prayer which closed it and then returned it to the Ark.

The following day we returned to our camp from the excitement of wartime Paris.

It was December 1918. The war was over. Because of the salvage plan we had developed, our area was in perfect order, and the inspector general gave us a top rating. There was nothing for me to do, but still I had to stay with the division.

Then a telegram arrived informing me of the death of my father—shocking news because there had been no warning. My father was only fifty-two and had been in apparent good health up to two days before his death. Also, while Cayce had repeatedly assured me that no harm would come to me physically, I had not asked him for readings on the members of the family, and, when in trance, Cayce responded only to what he was asked; the forces on which he drew, from wherever they came, did not volunteer information when they spoke through the sleeping man.

I went to General Smith, explained about the death of my father, pointed out that everything here was in apple-pie order, and asked his permission to go home by the earliest available transportation. General Smith told me, "I am sorry about your father's death, but you are a soldier. You've seen death in many forms. You are not going home until the division goes."

In my opinion, I had a right to get home. And with the war over, a right to try to achieve the goal in any honorable way. I thought of Judge's injunction—go to the top—and decided I would write to the commander-in-chief of our expeditionary forces, General Pershing. But I would send the letter through channels. This was entirely legal under military protocol and regulations. General Smith could disapprove it, but he had to forward it under regulations.

Knowing that General Pershing was a Mason, I reminded him that whenever a Mason was down to his last penny he could apply to a fellow Mason for help and consideration. I told him that symbolically on that basis I was requesting the general's help in obtaining immediate return to the United States. "I have eight younger brothers and sisters, my father has just died, and my mother needs me. The war is over and my duty has been performed. . . ."

The letter went through regular channels; but a carbon copy of the letter went to General Pershing's headquarters. Two days later, I received a telegram from the army chief-of-staff ordering me to the United States, with least possible delay and in the quickest manner possible.

General Smith was not too happy. Nevertheless, there were my official orders from General Pershing's office and he had to turn them over to me. When I got to Brest, my port of embarkation for America, however, I learned that there were still orders for me to stay in Europe—this time as a loading officer on the Brest docks.

I was able, however, to arrange the work details so that I did get home—all in the line of loading materials for shipment—without having a three-month delay on the docks of Brest, France.

As soon as our ship reached America, I sent telegrams to my mother and to Cayce. Then I reported as ordered to the office of the chief-of-staff in Washington. The colonel I talked with knew all about me. I had helped train his brother-in-law to become a second lieutenant back in Fort Worth, and he had been trying to locate me all over Europe, he told me. Then he added, "When that message from you came to Pershing appealing to him as a Mason, it was I who said you merited consideration. Otherwise, you'd have been court-martialed because even though it was on a carbon, it looked like you were sending a letter over your own general's head."

Despite this near disaster—which had turned out well only because of that coincidence of the colonel being in Pershing's headquarters—the Cayce prophecy had been fulfilled: I had gone in honor and come in honor.

Aware of my family problems, the colonel gave me a wide-ranging assignment to tour the Southern states and report to him on various detailed tasks he gave or would give to me from time to time. I was virtually a free agent.

Mourning the loss of my father and grieved that I was not able to be there at the time of need, I was glad to be home at last. Mother's problems worried me most. The grocery business continued—on a reduced scale. But she had the burden of the remaining outstanding obligations my father left by his sudden death.

Many of the small planters, black and white, had been at the funeral services for my father. They regarded him as a true friend in the deepest, most meaningful sense of that word.

Not long after the services, a Negro planter came to see my mother. He raised wheat and corn and ultimately did quite well financially. He said my father had lent him three thousand dollars without a note, and now, since my father was dead and the planter had no pressing financial problems as perhaps my mother did, he wanted to pay it back. He gave her his check for three thousand dollars.

My mother always insisted there was never a time when she was in need; when she got into difficult situations, God always helped her.

Nevertheless, my father's death presented many terrible problems for the family. It came so swiftly that he had had no time to set his affairs in any order whatsoever. As always over the years, he had a great many customers on a credit basis; otherwise, these tobacco planters and small farmers could not have survived. He was running a personal credit system and hundreds of dollars were owed, but times were hard and there was no money, the war was over, and my father was gone.

We owned nearly seventy-five parcels of land and buildings, but the banks were about to seek court orders that these properties be sold to clear up outstanding indebtedness. I called Judge about the situation and had a reading that advised us not to dispose of the property. I decided to remain in the active reserve of the Army because as long as I did this, no one could take away any property from us to pay for debts outstanding. Then I began to set up arrangements to pay off the debts out of earnings of our properties in the future. I also set up a procedure whereby each younger member of the family, as he became of legal age, signed an agreement to assume his share of this responsibility.

At this somewhat shadowed passage of our stars, both Cayce and I were in financial difficulties. I had to make a great deal of money to pay off those debts. They totaled around sixty-five thousand dollars. Cayce knew now the work that he wanted most of all to do was to use his gift, this ability to diagnose physical illness and health, and to help guide others by means of the readings.

He was dreaming of a hospital, a place of doctors and trained personnel who would work in cooperation with the readings Cayce was able to give. It would be a laboratory, a testing ground of Cayce's powers and of what was sure to become known as parapsychological factors in healing. All doctors and physicians, surgeons and serious students of all kinds—scoffers and believers alike—would be welcome there. It would be a place where they could give the treatments as described in readings—but under full medical and nursing administration. They would be able to give patients the right diets, the right treatments—medical, electrical, and osteopathic.

All this, of course, would cost much money, and Cayce therefore was eager to talk to me about it because of the widespread development of newly opened-up oil fields. Cayce said we should go to Texas and investigate the possibility of getting oil leases. Tremendous fortunes were being made in those days in the developing of Texas oil fields. It must be remembered that Cayce, however brilliant he was in the knowledge of readings, had limited understanding of technical subjects and even less of business and industry. This was one reason I set myself up at that time as a protector against those who would use Judge—and possibly harm or destroy him. We talked long into the night about these ideas.

We talked about money. He said the money wasn't for himself, but if we had enough, we would run the hospital free to all who came.

I told him there was plenty of money and oil available. "I've got friends all over the East, North, South," I told Judge. "I can get backers for us."

We talked about where we could raise funds, individuals to whom we could turn. Nobody in the world could stop us now. Of that we were sure. But dreams—even with Cayce—had to be shaped finally in hard reality.

In Lexington, Cayce and I talked with a lawyer about leases on Texas property where we might want to make borings. The lawyer gave us information that he said was Texas law. Cayce wanted us to use a ninety-nine-year lease form and this lawyer pointed out that Cayce knew nothing about the law while he, on the other hand, was a Texas lawyer and a member of the bar in Fort Worth. Cayce, he said, was totally wrong on certain legal points regarding the ninety-nine-year leases in Texas.

The lawyer stood firm on this. At my suggestion, Cayce went

into a hypnotic sleep, and we had a reading on it. The reading said, "You go to Frankfort, capital of Kentucky, and there in the archives you will find the statutes of the state of Texas and this information is available." Still in hypnotic sleep on the floor, he gave the page number on which the correct information about the lease was to be found.

The lawyer was so infuriated that he told us he would prove once and for all that Cayce was wrong. He got on a bus and went to Frankfort. Hours later, the lawyer phoned back. Obviously shaken, he admitted that Cayce, in his hypnotic sleep, had correctly cited the page on which the fact bearing out Cayce's reading was found.

It seemed a good omen, that lawyer calling back from Frankfort to verify Cayce's reading on lease laws. It pointed to an adventure we were about to share. One that presented perils and pitfalls, but also a promise of flowing black gold with which we would pay off debts and build a great hospital to serve humanity.

But the oil-drenched dreams of Cayce and myself were not to turn out as we two fervently desired.

The forces had other plans.

CHAPTER 5

"Be You Oil Men . . . I'll Kill You . . ."

A few days before I arrived back in the States, Cayce had received a letter from the editor of the Cleveland *Daily News,* a Mr. D. M. Thrash, who had heard of Cayce's powers. He and some of his associates wanted Cayce to come to Cleveland, the editor said. He wanted him to look over the Sam Davis Oil Company in which a group of them had invested. They wanted him to give them readings about oil.

It was this letter—not a reading—which gave Cayce the idea that oil might provide an answer to his need of large sums of money to build his hospital.

There was nothing wrong in raising funds, nor could I see anything wrong in using Cayce's gift as a part of the process of raising money for such a cause as his. Moreover, there were many people who appeared willing to help us, to provide funds for borings and testing for oil fields—provided Cayce would give information through his readings.

We were both too inexperienced and naive—perhaps also too eager and too hungry—to realize that we were moving into a world alien to all of Cayce's ideals and gifts, a world of violence, greed, deceit, and sabotage.

We did not believe, nor was there any hint in the readings, that this was *not* the path intended as "we" were neutral. Judge and I would have to discover for ourselves. In Texas, Cayce would give geological readings constantly. He would tell us what was in the earth, deep down in the earth, more accurately than the geologists could. But in this instance at least—perhaps because we *had* moved into an aura of violence—he did not always see what was in the hearts of those around us.

There were underlying reasons that led Cayce into this somewhat unusual—even bizarre—psychic side road.

The early adult years had been difficult ones for Cayce, particularly in finances. He was not a businessman or of a creative business mind. He had other troubles, too. His wife, Gertrude Evans Cayce, had been a tremendous help to him in running the photography business. They had their son, Hugh Lynn Cayce, but had lost their second boy in infancy in 1911. Later Edgar Evans Cayce was born in 1918. And Gertrude herself had become ill with tuberculosis. Again, with all his ability to help others, it had seemed impossible for him to help himself or his wife. Finally, in a reading, he gave a series of medical prescriptions with a number of doctors sitting in the room listening.

The doctors neither understood nor accepted these prescriptions. Part of the treatment was to put apple brandy in a charred oak keg and let Gertrude inhale the fumes. Another part included putting a number of drugs in a capsule and giving it to his wife in a liquid. So close to death was Gertrude, however, that although the doctors did not understand or approve of his suggestions, they agreed to try Cayce's improbable prescriptions. The alternative was to sit back and let her die.

Thomas Sugrue in his book about Cayce entitled *There Is*

a River described that moment in the Cayce story: "Jackson (one of the doctors) told Gertrude he wanted her to do what the readings suggested. She was too weak to resist or care. She could barely raise her head from the pillow. After the first capsule she ceased to have hemorrhages. After the second day her fever disappeared. The fumes of the apple brandy helped the congestion in her lungs. Very slowly she gained strength, falling again and again into relapse. . . ."

The readings continued, and gradually the moments of weakness and relapse grew more infrequent until she was on the road to full recovery.

Those first years had been times of trouble, uncertainty, and indecision about his career and future. Should he remain in his photography business and on the side carry on his readings—for which he received no money at all? Or should he give up one or the other entirely?

Gertrude was his guide, his mentor, the focal point of most of his life. She ran the photographic studio he had set up when they moved to Selma. She handled sittings and customers and billings; she kept tabs on his outside work for companies, particularly for one large Southern railway line that he represented photographically for years.

Judge was a sensitive photographer. His pictures were widely used by the railroad in various publications and promotional materials. The trouble was that his interests were divided. He had to become one thing or another; he could not be both. That was why the plan for the hospital—and the concept of obtaining funds from oil to bring it into reality—marked one of the most critical decisions of his life.

In the weeks we were together talking over these plans, I became ever closer to this family—to Gertrude, to Judge's sister Annie, and to the other sisters. Judge and I were pals—we liked to laugh, to fish, to talk, and to tell stories. To stroll the streets of Selma, Alabama, where he was living. Or to watch a parade with Edgar Evans on my shoulders so he could see over the heads of the crowd.

Judge enjoyed sitting back and telling stories of his cases: the readings he gave while unconscious often astounded him as much as they did others. In those early days, I took down hundreds of those early readings myself. Sometimes his answers to a situation sounded literally impossible. A man whose sister had been confined to a mental institution wanted to know what was really wrong with her. Doctors had been unable to find the cause of her mental breakdown or what to do about it.

Cayce's reading said the woman had an impacted wisdom tooth and that this condition was affecting the brain. "Take a picture," the reading stated, "and you will see it; remove it, and she will get well."

Pull a wisdom tooth—to cure insanity? The treatment itself sounded insane. Yet within a few months, the woman was fully restored to health and later became an assisting nurse to a local doctor, a position she held for some years.

There were always new cases, new people, and their needs. But for Cayce and me, the gushing promise of the Texas oil appeared to hold the answers to all needs.

We met with the people in Cleveland and funds were provided by various interested individuals to reactivate the Sam Davis Oil Company. Cayce agreed to be a part of the plan and to give readings. The money for leases and exploration was put up by a number of wealthy people in Ohio, Georgia, Kentucky, and Texas. They were all amateurs. Their faith in the Sam Davis Oil Company lay basically in the psychic role to be played by Cayce.

With several other associates, Cayce and I went first to Comanche County, Texas, where the readings said positively that oil would be found. Cayce's fourteen-year-old son, Hugh Lynn, was with us. We had tools and equipment, which we brought with us from Ardmore, Oklahoma, where we also contacted professional drillers and other workers who joined us.

Our rights were to the oil underneath fields where Cayce gave readings. Cayce gave these readings right on the spot. The readings said there was oil ready to flow. Geologists couldn't tell for sure that there was oil there—but Cayce predicted that we would hit it. We began to drill. There is on record an affidavit by one of the drillers, telling how Cayce knew in advance what every layer of underlying rock formation and sand would contain, how far down we would have to go, and similar factual data about which he himself had no knowledge whatsoever, technical or otherwise. One morning the drillers told us we had reached the oil-bearing sands. That afternoon we saw gushing over the derrick a mixture of water and oil, indicating that we were close to a real strike.

That night we lost a string of tools. We began to encounter other difficulties which delayed us. Granite blocks were dropped into the drill hole by persons unknown, and it became apparent that someone wanted us out. Many millions of dollars were at stake—but our funds were almost gone.

Cayce's reading had been right. The oil, as the reading had said, was there. But the brutal realities of the oil fields, about which we had not questioned Cayce, had been disastrous for our plans.

Cayce was not there all the time, but he made a number of trips back and forth, and he was always available if needed. He came in now to give us encouragement. After we had managed to raise enough funds to begin again, a reading advised that we seek a new location. It said that we should start looking near a place called Luling, Texas, not far from San Antonio.

While mesmerized in a trance, he said we were to go to the county seat of Luling, and we would meet on the steps of the courthouse a man who would tell us where the oil was and how to locate it. However incredible it sounded, a few days later Cayce and I went down to Luling.

It was like acting in a play in which I knew exactly what was about to happen. When we got to the courthouse, I saw an elderly man coming down the steps carrying a cane. I went up to him and I said, "Pardon me, sir, my name is David E. Kahn, and I am here investigating any possible oil formation in this area."

His answer was, "Well, you couldn't have picked a better man."

He explained that he was a county judge. He had lived in the area many years and knew its formations intimately, as well as its archives and records. He thought we were on the track of a real find and suggested a site some miles out of town. He also told me that I should go into a building directly across the street and down a long hall to the office of the state geologist. So Cayce and I and another man from our group went over to talk to the geologist.

The young geologist told us about the area we were interested in. A white woman in that area had by a series of purchases obtained a large tract of property most of which had previously been owned by largely impoverished Negroes. She was, it appeared, a dominant figure—although white—throughout this area of poor blacks. Moreover, he said, she took a protective role toward the blacks, and we would probably be unable to do business with her. She kept a shotgun close by the front door.

We drove out there to what they called the farm and knocked on the front door of the house. A gun was poked out and the woman's voice said, "Be you oil men . . . I'll kill you."

I told her I was an army man, gave her our names, and explained that I was from Kentucky.

The woman opened the door a little more, peered at me and demanded, "What part of Kentucky?"

"Lexington."

The door opened wider. There I saw this aging, barefoot woman standing in rags, gray-haired, wrinkled face, holding her gun at us. Slightly more respectfully, she asked, "You know a man named Phillips?"

I said I did and she said, "What does he look like?"

I described him and explained he was a druggist in Lexington, and the woman said, "He's my brother."

I said she could send a telegram to her brother and ask him how long he had known me and in the meantime we were hungry from the long drive and was there anywhere around we could get a bite to eat? To that she replied, "I don't have no money and I don't have no food."

I told her to go to the grocery store and get eggs, butter, bread, and coffee and then go to the telegraph office in the village nearby and send a telegram to her brother. She agreed. Phillips later confirmed our friendship.

When she returned from the village, I asked her about her own health. She said she had not been in good health for a long time. Her son had tuberculosis and she had brought him out here where it was dry so that she could cure his condition. "But now he is in Kansas City and I am here protecting these poor colored people from the oil swindlers."

I told her frankly that we were there to find oil. I told her about Cayce and his readings, and how he told us we would find oil in this area.

"Well, there's lot of oil around here," she said. "And they don't have to drill more than a hundred feet to get it. On rainy days, the cattle won't drink the water, there is so much oil on top of it."

I said I wanted to talk about that but first why not let Mr. Cayce give her a reading. So we put newspapers on the floor because there was no floor covering and Judge stretched out on his back on the newspapers. I gave him the name of the woman and the signal to go to sleep.

As he followed my instructions, I gave the further order, "Please give me a physical, mental, and spiritual reading and tell us if she has any troubles and what they are and what to do for them."

He began to tell her about her physical condition. And this disheveled old woman, who was watching Judge very intently, began to cry and said, "I never saw anything like this in my whole life." She said he'd told her exactly what was wrong and what to get to help it and this was the most wonderful thing that had ever happened to her.

She began to talk about the oil in the ground that she was holding for the blacks and said that maybe we could help. Maybe Mr. Cayce could give a reading about the oil and how much there was and how to handle it.

We all went outside the house then, and Judge stretched out right on the ground and the reading he gave told of a fabulous fortune, a sea of oil directly underneath him.

Nearby was a dead tree, with two prongs of the trunk sticking up against the Texas sky. Cayce, lying in hypnotic trance, about thirty feet from the tree, said, "If you will drill under the tree you will get oil within three hundred feet but you will also get oil throughout the area. It is a great salt dome loaded with the richest oil in Texas."

We made an agreement with her and gave her a flat sum of a few hundred dollars out of my army pay to make the deal. She trusted us and we did not betray that trust. She and the people on that land were protected in their rights, and we were given rights to bring in the wells. We had a five-year lease on three thousand acres, for which we had to pay a dollar per acre per year. Of course, we had to pay all expenses of drilling. Seven-eighths of any profits obtained were ours; the rest went to her and the black people. This was a standard agreement for those who drilled—and those who held the land.

Once again we ran into difficulties; some of the drillers

seemed to be with us and some were not. Various individuals and groups moved in and out of the area, working with us at times and drifting off to other fields. There were problems, antagonisms, competition; the greed that was almost lust for oil became a desperate all-consuming thing. There was sabotage here too. Wreckage. And in the end no more funds.

Our quest next led us to San Saba County. In addition to being a rich oil-prospecting area, it was a mirror of all the wildness and wonder of Texas and the Southwest. The primitive out-of-doors life of the plains provided us with temporary escape from the problems and antagonisms which were slowly destroying our work. Although still on active reserve with occasional special assignments from the Army, I spent much time in this area. Cayce and Hugh Lynn, then a teen-ager, were frequently with me to share the adventure of this land. I often carried a loaded .45 automatic in my holster. We traveled across some of the great grazing ranches. There was one ranch that covered hundreds of thousands of acres. You could ride for a week and still be on the same land. There was a big lake on this ranch, and Judge and I would get up at five o'clock in the morning and go fishing for bass. One morning Judge caught a seven-pound bass with a bamboo rod with a string attached to it. He cleaned it and put corn meal on it, and we fried it ourselves, and nobody ever ate a fish more delicious than that.

Hugh Lynn watched the Texas cowhands with fascination. Some of their horses were only half broken to the saddle and rider, but Hugh Lynn wanted to ride, too. The first time he got into the saddle, he let loose the reins and off went his horse across fields and over fences. Some of the regular hands took off after him in a real cowboy movie chase. They finally caught up with him and brought the runaway to a halt.

One of the cowboys told Hugh Lynn he'd do better when he got the knack of it. Erect in the saddle, proud of the fact that he hadn't fallen off, Hugh Lynn reportedly answered,

"Mister, maybe I didn't know the knack before this ride, but I sure do now."

But here in San Saba, our oil experience followed the same pattern. Once again, borings were tampered with and made useless, tools were ruined, all our efforts wasted—and all our funds used up. Judge could tell us where the oil was, but we could not deal with the oil field world in which we were operating. It was a rugged, dangerous cosmos of good and evil, of scientists and businessmen, of promoters, operators, freebooters, killers. We had friends who relied on us and on whom we could rely—friends whose goals were the same as ours—but we were also locked in an area that was alien to much of our earlier lives and particularly alien to the psychic gifts of Edgar Cayce.

Yet it had been his suggestion that we become involved in this and that he use his power to find oil so that he could obtain funds for his hospital. From this experience we learned much not only about ourselves and the others involved, but more important, about the nature of the readings themselves. Edgar Cayce, through his psychic gift, could help others—it seemed he could always help others. But helping himself, for whatever purpose, was another matter. Awake and thinking, he was just another speculator with tall plans and short funds. He could make all the mistakes of any average man. He allowed a Cayce Petroleum Company to be formed and it bought in and out of operations with others, but in the end it did not produce very much for anyone—and nothing for Cayce or myself.

Many times as we talked together about some of the problems and conflicting ideas, he would express his opinion. But I would say, "Judge, let's wait. Let's get a reading on it." And many times, indeed as often as not, the readings Cayce gave would completely reverse his waking self.

Even more important, Cayce had said that the readings were merely a channel through which information may come. It was his conviction that their source was the ultimate good and that they should, indeed could, be used only for good. So many people had become involved in this enterprise and their purposes and motivations varied widely. For every one who was truly dedicated to the establishment of the hospital, to the best possible use of Cayce's gift, there was another whose only goal was profit. In this atmosphere of confusion, disagreement, and greed the information provided by the readings, however accurate, could come to nothing.

By now we had nearly reached the end of our venture. One last episode remained. Among the oddly assorted group of men —investors, hangers-on and drillers—who were with us at that time, some openly resented me and my close association with Cayce.

One man, a huge individual, accused me of trying to take the lion's share of all of whatever we might get. There came a night when some of these fellows charged that I was about to grab the whole thing. Actually, we had nothing to take; everything we had left at that time was going into trying to reach a real bonanza.

I couldn't just let these attacks and accusations erode everything. I told them all that there was a simple way to establish the facts. We were all aware of Judge's abilities. At eight o'clock the following night, I said, we would have a reading. Everyone would be present. I would answer any and all questions about my part in this operation. I would submit to this. And Cayce's readings would either bear out what I said or prove me a liar.

That night Cayce lay down on his back on the floor and before I could say anything, or give him a suggestion, he was asleep. He had passed that moment just as his eyelids flickered; closed, then opened again, at which he could receive proper suggestions; he had fallen into a regular sleep and there would be no response to questions.

I had a feeling that perhaps that night Judge really wanted, secretly, unconsciously, to escape from these animosities that encircled him. He knew the greed on all sides; they were expecting him to lead them into vast riches. And that was all. "They don't care about the hospital, or my work, or anything else I stand for," Judge told me on several occasions. "All they want is to get rich. . . ."

He had every reason that night to want to escape from this roomful of suspicion and hate. But when he went into that sudden sleep before I could give one instruction, I was deeply concerned. No word, no response, nothing.

The others sat there grimly, watching, waiting. The great man who could answer all the questions about David Kahn's real intentions and purposes could now say nothing at all. Cayce lay there on the floor, motionless, wordless. The silence in the room was almost overwhelming.

Shortly after eight o'clock I told everyone there to go to bed or get out or whatever they wanted to do but to leave me and Mr. Cayce alone.

I didn't want to call a doctor because he would not know what this was all about and I did not know what accusations might be made or what harm a doctor who didn't know what he was dealing with might do to Cayce.

Judge was in trouble and I had to help him, I had to work it out myself. I was the only one in the group who knew how to put him into this sleep in any case. Every ten minutes I tried to wake him through the usual suggestions but without success.

Because of the nature of the kind of sleep that he went into there was always a potential danger. The forces he dealt with are little understood, even now. As the hours ticked past, and I still could not arouse him, my apprehension increased.

I was in a panic. I would do anything to help this motionless man on the floor. Yet calling the authorities could do greater harm than not calling them, might even cost his life. Alone there, in the oppressive, seemingly endless silence of the Texas night, I realized that I was responsible, I had let him get into this. I did not know where I had lost control of the situation but I had.

Then I remembered the fact that Cayce usually slept for eight hours when he went into normal sleep. He had gone to sleep in this instance just before eight o'clock. I got an alarm clock and set it to go off at four o'clock.

Then I sat and waited. The only sound in the room was the ticking of that clock. Alone in this room with my sleeping friend, I waited.

Precisely at four o'clock, with a startling shrill jangle, the alarm went off. For a moment Judge lay there unresponsive. Then—one moment later—he jumped up to his feet, fully awake, fully normal, demanding to know what was the matter.

"Judge," I told him, "you went to sleep and never said a word."

He was greatly upset. He knew something had happened, but didn't know what. Why hadn't he been able to give the reading? It was to him a disturbing, frightening disorientation. I sat with him for over an hour and we talked about it.

I told him how I had made the men go and how they had left one at a time so as not in any way to disturb or endanger him. He was bitterly disappointed with these men around us. He said they were thinking only about the hundreds of barrels a day of oil Cayce had said could come out of the fields—if we were able to fund the operations, which we were not able to do. They did not care about the hospital. In the back of their minds, he said, they were thinking to hell with it, to hell with the hospital. They didn't give a damn about it. They wanted only to use him for themselves.

I had told the men to come back the following night at the same time. We went through the whole day with considerable uncertainty and uneasiness. There were many possibilities as to why Cayce had not been able to give the reading. My belief was that it was the atmosphere of distrust and animosity engendered by all the arguments. Now it would all come out in the open.

He went into his sleep that next evening under my direction and answered all the questions I put to him for the men—any questions they wanted to ask. The answers he gave each of them were almost like individual readings. They were portraits of distrust and suspicion and the underlying greed in some of these people.

I had been the one directly accused of wanting to grab the whole thing. The reading gave me complete exoneration. It said I had no such ideas or plans. I was only anxious to see the hospital succeed and to pay off debts at home. That was what the reading said.

But afterward, when Judge and I went over the whole situation, I think we both knew even then, although it was to be some months before we gave up entirely, that these activities were not for him, not for us.

It was clear that this episode, with all its terror and underlying patterns of hate, was a symbol of a world to which we did not belong.

The mystic can see beyond the horizons for others—not often for himself. Within a few months, we had run out of money again. A year later we were forced to give up our lease. At the Fort Worth Club, I met a man named Edgar B. Davis, owner of a rubber business in Massachusetts. Davis was a man who also had psychic gifts and heard prophecies. He later became famous by bringing to Broadway a play about reincarnation called *The Ladder*. There was no charge for admission. Davis kept the play going for several years—out of his own funds.

Once in Fort Worth Davis told me that one of his voices had instructed him to come to Luling to find oil. A year and a half after we had to surrender our lease there because of lack of funds, I received a newspaper clipping from Davis with the headline: LULING TEXAS AFLOW.

This was the property that Judge—in trance outside the old woman's shack—had described as holding a sea of oil.

Davis had obtained the rights we had to let go. According to the best reports I received, he had drilled fourteen wells, all of which had come in. He sold the property we had been forced to surrender for twelve million dollars.

CHAPTER 6

A Cinder in His Eye

Our efforts in the oil fields covered many months; both Cayce and I made a number of trips together back and forth during those years, usually by train. Some of these adventures ran concurrently with our adventures in the oil fields. Some of them were concerned not with the oil nor with the dream of the hospital, but directly with Judge's tremendous diagnostic gifts.

One of the most significant extra-curricular experiences of that whole period of our lives began with a cinder in Cayce's eye.

We were coming, on that occasion, from Birmingham into Nashville, Tennessee, on the train, and as the eye was inflamed and painful, I suggested that we get off and find a doctor. We called the conductor, reclaimed our tickets so that we could complete our journey later—every penny counted in those days—grabbed our baggage, and jumped off just as the train was starting to pull out of the Nashville station.

I got out the classified phone book and to my astonishment discovered in the list of physicians a Dr. E. B. Cayce. I reached him on the phone and told him the situation. I don't think Judge and he were related; if they were it was distant. But Dr.

Cayce said he would be delighted to remove the cinder from Edgar Cayce's eye.

We found him to be a charming gentleman who was amazed to learn—and from me of course—who this other Cayce was, and what he did. Dr. Cayce was so enthralled he asked us if we would care to delay our already interrupted journey long enough to have lunch with him at the Union League Club.

On reaching the table at the club we found that we were sitting with six prominent businessmen of the city, including a banker, a real estate tycoon, the president of a railroad, and the owner of Nashville's leading newspaper. Dr. Cayce introduced us. There was much discussion about the coincidence of names.

Judge never talked much about himself but I didn't hesitate to tell these men some of Cayce's experiences and the readings I had heard him give.

As a result of that luncheon, we remained for about two weeks as Dr. Cayce's guests in Nashville. Many readings were given. Families and individuals would come to him. Many were helped or guided by the things he told them.

A dramatic demonstration of Cayce's forces occurred before a group of doctors on this visit to Nashville. In Birmingham, from which we had arrived, we had also made many friends and given readings, without charge or fee. I wanted Cayce to make friends everywhere. I wanted people to meet, know, and like him. I wanted to make his work and worth known.

One of the group we had met in Birmingham telephoned us in Nashville in an emergency. At the time of the call, we were in a meeting set up by a man named William Rosenblum, who later became a rabbi and served at Temple Israel in New York City. At that time he was a lawyer interested in many Nashville activities. Cayce's arrival in town had caught his attention and he had brought a large group of physicians and friends to witness and hear a psychic reading.

When the phone call came, the available information was extremely meager. A young woman who attended our meetings in Birmingham had been told in a reading by Cayce that she was in love with a young newspaperman, but there had been a disagreement. Now it appeared from the long-distance call to Nashville that she had swallowed some kind of poison and was critically ill.

The group in Nashville was now much more interested in the phone call than in anything I could say. Judge promptly stretched out in front of the doctors and at my suggestion went to sleep. Cayce stated in the reading that the girl had taken bichloride of mercury. He described exactly what she should do as a counter-measure; the antidote given was itself another extremely toxic liquid. Cayce also stated in the reading that the body would not survive unless the prescription given in the reading was followed. In front of the group in Nashville, I phoned this information to Birmingham. They heard me confirm on the phone the fact that it was bichloride of mercury the girl had taken, although the original message had not specified the drug.

Everyone at the Nashville meeting heard the Cayce reading. And the warning. But the doctors in Birmingham refused to give another poison as had been suggested in Judge's reading, even though they apparently did not have any other antidote. Whatever treatment they tried, it did not succeed. The young girl died three days later.

The tragedy to me was that nothing else they tried had proved effective in saving her life. And Cayce's suggestions were simply dismissed. The importance of the long-distance telephone reading, however, was that it demonstrated to a large gathering including medical men that Cayce was able to diagnose a patient in Birmingham without knowing any of her symptoms.

We had not one but many meetings in Nashville with the doctors, and many times Judge's work was challenged. In one instance, he gave a reading with about eight physicians present. In another room was a patient whom neither Cayce nor I had seen, and about whom we knew nothing. At my suggestion, Cayce went into sleep and gave the reading. When he finished, the doctor, without indicating how accurate Judge was, said, "Tell me something about the patient I *don't* know."

"Mr. Cayce," I said, "will you go over the body again and see if there is anything on this body that you have not discussed and tell the doctor."

"Yes," came the response. "In between two toes there is a rash—and that just came."

Still in trance, he described the nature of the rash and told them what to do about it. And then he added, "That, the doctor doesn't know."

Without a word, the doctor left the room to investigate this claim. On his return after examining his patient, the physician told those present: "He does have a rash between his toes. It was not there when I examined him three or four days ago."

Another surprising episode in Nashville grew out of a reading Cayce had given for a young girl. When he finished, one of the doctors commented that it did sound as if Cayce in the reading had actual information, but the doctor added that he disagreed with Cayce's diagnosis.

When I relayed this to Cayce, the response came, "Well, he won't agree also that there's a scar on the bottom of the girl's foot because he's never seen it, but if he examines under the big toe he'll find it there. It was caused by stepping on a hot cinder when she was a little girl, and the scar is still there. She knows it but he doesn't." This odd and insignificant physical detail was confirmed by examination and by the young lady herself.

The Nashville doctors did not dispute the fact that these were valid readings, that they contained technical details about which Cayce could not have known and even facts which the doctors themselves had not known about their own patients. But the physicians had developed their own explanation for the Cayce phenomena. Cayce, they said, had a limited education, didn't read books except for the Bible, had no medical knowledge and had *never* studied medicine. "But you, Kahn, do read books and do have an education. You know all these things and you read up on the cases and all he does is read your mind."

This theory at least had originality. I explained first that I would have to have an extraordinary memory to keep hundreds of medical cases in my mind, especially since I didn't read medical books, didn't know anything about medicine beyond the usual popular medical terms, and had never studied medicine. And even if I had some medical knowledge, how could I diagnose a case directly without seeing the patient? Moreover, if I could hold information in my mind and Cayce could read it directly, that in itself would be a miracle beyond anything known to science or psychiatry. I added, however, that he wasn't reading my mind. Usually, I never even met the patients. And Cayce would not allow families or physicians or anyone else to tell him anything about the cases beyond the name and address of the patient.

"If you're honest in giving the proper name and location of the patient," I said, "you will get a diagnosis and you can ask questions about it and get an answer. But it has nothing to do with me; he did his readings before he met me, and there is nothing in my educational background that permits him to get from me all this information about medicine or science or literature or art or psychology or philosophy, which he seems very adept in when he's asleep. When he is awake, he can't even spell the word 'asafetida'—and neither can I. But when we asked him in his sleep how to spell it, he told us where to find it in the book, what page it was on, and he spelled it."

I told them, also, that if they could explain how this was

done, they could probably resolve a great many other doubts and reservations in their own minds about this man and his work.

To Judge, the people who called on his help were not cases, but individuals, these people who simply had not been able to get help elsewhere. One woman had been married ten years but had no children. Doctors had been unable to determine the cause. She asked for a reading. As a protection for all concerned in such a delicate situation, since she could not bring her husband with her, I suggested that, if not her husband, she at least bring some older person with her.

She did. She brought along her very charming eighty-year-old grandmother.

The reading was given in the usual way. The question was simply why she could have no children and whether it was her fault or her husband's. Cayce went into a long physical discussion in the reading. In the usual phraseology of the reading he found the "body"—the subject—in the room and that the body had been injured riding horseback. Apparently this had happened some time before. Judge said that the injury had pushed her pelvic organs out of place. He said that the husband was in good health and was not responsible for the situation.

He went on to state that the wife should go to an osteopath and have the condition corrected. In detail he described how this could be done. He then told the woman that if she did this she would have a child within the year.

Both the woman and her husband came from leading Nashville families. The wife did exactly as Cayce's reading had told her to do. We were informed later that she became pregnant approximately three months later. The baby was born within the time the reading prophesied.

Our adventures in that unsettled, highly mobile period of our lives ranged over thousands of miles. When we realized after months that our Texas dreams had all run dry, Judge went back to Selma to return to photography and to think over new plans for the hospital and the future of his psychic work, which he was not prepared to give up.

It took longer for me to drain the oil out of my mind and activities. I was not quite ready to quit. Alone I went out to Denver, Colorado, where I worked for a prominent lawyer who was also an oil man interested in a number of tracts. His name was B. D. Townsend and through him I met some of the most influential citizens of Denver, including a man named Frederick Gilmer Bonfils, publisher of the Denver *Post*.

Townsend thought that Mr. Bonfils would be an excellent person for Cayce to meet because the paper could use stories about him. Bonfils said he would like to have Cayce come out and give him a reading. Bonfils agreed to pay all expenses. Cayce, virtually broke as usual, came out. He and Mr. Townsend and I went to see Bonfils, in his private office at the Denver *Post*.

Cayce stretched out on the office couch and gave a reading about Bonfil's condition. Bonfils walked up and down with great agitation and whenever Judge would name some part of the body and describe its condition Bonfils would put his hand to that spot. When the reading was over, Bonfils said, "This is the finest thing I have ever seen." And he told Judge, "You know what I am going to do with you? If you will follow suggestions, we will become partners."

Cayce's eyes watched the man but otherwise gave no indication of how he was reacting. Bonfils continued, "We'll make Kahn the general manager, and our friend Townsend general counselor. I will direct the operation."

His enthusiasm grew as he began to race through the plans he was making. "I will buy you a white specially made Cadillac or Packard. We'll dress you in a white silk costume with a turban and I will make the appointments, two a day. You'll get a thousand dollars for the one in the morning. The one you do in the afternoon belongs to me and you'll do the kind of reading I want.

"You'll have a reading scheduled for every day in the year. And you'll be scheduled for every movement you make, where you are to appear and before what groups you will speak. You will be nationally famous because we will headline you in the Denver *Post.*

"This," he said with a wave of his hands, "is going to begin immediately. I am willing to finance the operation and Mr. Townsend can draw up the necessary papers and details —and you and I are partners."

Judge, with an expression of utter calm, kept looking at Bonfils without saying a word until Bonfils finally said to him, "Well, what is your comment?"

Cayce answered very slowly, in his familiar Southern drawl, "I don't know, Mr. Bonfils. But there's one thing I can tell you. I'm not a showman. I'm not going to be portrayed as one. And I'm not wearing any turban because I am not what the turban says it is."

A silence came over the room. Bonfils and Cayce eyed each other steadily. Cayce said. "I'm a country boy from the Kentucky hills. I can give you a reading like you saw today and that's the way it has to be kept. I'm past and done with giving readings on horses or gambling or anything like that because it's only brought me trouble.

"If you want to keep this on the mental, physical, and spiritual basis, I'd be interested, if it helps humanity, or you, or the people who read your paper. But I don't want any white cars or costumes or personal fanfare. . . ."

He assured Bonfils, however, that he would give him or his family readings as long as it helped them. "I've turned down many offers to go on the stage and many offers from newspapers to buy my story."

Bonfils wasn't willing to surrender. "Well, think it over, Mr.

Cayce," he said, still confident. "Meanwhile, I'd like to arrange a reading in a couple of days for one of my children."

Judge did give a number of additional readings for Bonfils and his family and some of his friends. But that was all.

What Bonfils was offering Cayce was a chance to become a millionaire. A thousand dollars a day—seven days a week through the year—would have made him one of the highest-paid individuals in America at that time.

Judge knew this. But he also learned in the mud and ooze of the Texas oil fields that commercializing his gift, even for the highest causes, simply wouldn't work.

It was time to go back and begin again. We had our lives and our responsibilities to face. Months later—after giving up the Western adventure for good and coming home—I had a reading from Judge in which he told me about my success and my future in the business world. My future would be made not in oil, but in wood and metal.

I did not understand this, but I accepted it; whatever it implied, I would find the understanding later. In an earlier reading, I had been told that I would find this understanding when I went to the largest city in the world by a great body of water. This could mean one place only—New York City.

I arrived in New York on January 1, 1924. I had a bare fifty dollars in funds, so I borrowed three hundred dollars from the Masonic Temple.

I went to the McAlpin Hotel and walked up to the hotel desk. An elderly lady was there. I said good morning and told her that I was short of money and did not know anybody in New York. I was recently out of the Army and looking for a job. It was all absolutely true.

She said, "Why don't you stay here with us until you get a job?"

She also said there was a man who would be coming downstairs in a moment or so who had a ladies' ready-to-wear store and was opening up another one. His name was Sheineman. She introduced us. Mr. Sheineman asked me what my background was and I told him about the grocery and food business and my army experience.

He asked me if I would like to be a floor manager in the store that was just opening. I accepted. I went over with him and made a tour of the store, which years later was occupied by Weber and Heilbroner. He asked me, "Can you live on seventy-five dollars a week?"

I told him I could.

This was not metal and wood, the materials in which my future would lie because Judge had said so. This was ladies' ready-to-wear clothes. But I was in the largest city in the world, by a very large body of water called the Atlantic Ocean.

CHAPTER 7

"In Wood and Metal . . ."

The job in ladies' dresses was a stopgap; it kept me in funds until I was able to get something not merely better but something in line with Cayce's readings on my future. *In wood and metal.*

I discovered through a coincidence that Mr. Sheineman's advertising manager was a friend of a Janet Boskey, whom I had met with her husband at a Masonic gathering in New York City. Janet's uncle had married my aunt many years before in Germany. So in New York, I became friends with the Boskeys, and naturally I discussed with them my plans for my future career. I had been offered a chance by the president of one of the largest food wholesalers in the country, Frank Leggett, to manage their Pittsburgh office, dealing primarily with large institutions. It looked like a real possibility. But again, it did not fit in with Cayce's predictions.

When I mentioned the Leggett offer to Janet, she asked me why I had come to New York in the first place if I now planned to go to Pittsburgh. I explained about Cayce and his statement that I should go into the wood and metal business, and this apparently amused Janet.

She said, "What do you consider a wood and metal business to be?"

Having given it much thought already, I said, "Well, the furniture business has to use screws and wood, and that, I think, would qualify as wood and metal."

There was a pause. I looked at Janet and suddenly saw tears in her eyes.

I said, "What's the matter, Janet?"

"It's—wonderful," she told me. "My brother Ben bought a half interest in a furniture factory just a short time ago. And this Mr. Cayce sends you here and I meet you. This is almost unbelievable. I'll have you meet Ben next Sunday morning."

The following Sunday I met Janet's brother, Ben Lauterstein, at the Boskeys'. He was then president of the Federal Furniture Company, which owned several factories, including the Carolina Wood Products Company in Asheville, North Carolina. They made bedroom and dining room furniture and employed about three hundred people. There was no place for me in the sales organization, however, because Ben and his partner, Irving Isaacs, handled all the accounts for the New York City area plus the accounts in the fifteen warehouses they had around the country in major cities like Cleveland, Detroit, and others of similar size.

However, in addition to the Asheville plant, the Federal Furniture Company had a plant in Sheboygan, Wisconsin, which manufactured player-roll cabinets. Player-roll pianos were in great vogue at the time, and people needed cabinets in which to keep the rolls. The products they were turning out were not top quality, but Ben thought it might be a chance for me to promote the sale of that plant's products plus whatever other orders I could get—in areas not already covered by the firm's sales representatives. These player-roll cabinets, I realized, could be modified and improved in design to serve many other needs and purposes.

About the middle of March I called my mother in Kentucky and told her that I had a chance of going either into the grocery business or the furniture business. I reminded her of the readings I had had from Cayce. "By all means," she told me over the long-distance phone, "take the furniture business. We've had enough of groceries." So I went to work for Ben Lauterstein of the Federal Furniture Company. "We pay no salaries, only commissions," Ben said, "but we'll carry you for a month to give you time to get yourself organized."

They gave me the Lower East Side of New York City as my sales district. I couldn't sell in any of the big stores in midtown. Furthermore, the material coming out of most of Federal's plants was tied up by other salesmen or was too expensive for the Lower East Side. If I was going to succeed, I had to find some new approach. The furniture produced at Sheboygan was so awful none of the other salesmen would handle it. I called Judge long distance and got a reading about this plant and my relationship to it. The reading came back that Sheboygan looked all right; it would be a long haul, but it would work out.

In other readings Cayce told me I was to deal with music, furniture, and radio stores. Now I seemed headed in that direction. I recall one day seeing an advertisement stating that a sewing machine company wanted to put one of their new models in a cabinet in such a way that the sewing machine could be used on the cabinet and folded out of sight when not in use. I cabled and put in a bid.

The company ordered a thousand cabinets, and we made a ten-dollar profit on each one. These cabinets were made at one of our company plants in Missouri. I could not use Sheboygan because they were not then geared for this type of production. The cabinets created a storm of excitement when they were shipped into town—a brand-new type of sewing machine. And I said, "We're in business—the metal machine, the wooden cabinet."

Meanwhile, I went out to Sheboygan and worked with their plant managers and their designers to improve its operation and production so I could sell some of their player-roll cabinets in New York City. The low-grade product with bubbles in the varnish was to be replaced by a sturdy mahogany cabinet with a top-quality finish.

I know that a number of those men wondered whatever had led me to believe I could do so much with these products. I did not tell them about the reading. They certainly were surprised with the results.

I went to Hearn's department store to talk with their buyers. Of course, I didn't know anyone in the store. I went up to one buyer with a pin in his lapel, and I said, "I see you wear a Legion pin."

He saw my button and said, "Wait over there." When the other commission salesmen had gone, he came over, and we talked about our army careers, and I laid out the pictures I had of the Sheboygan furniture. I said, "I can give you the combination player-roll cabinet and bookcase for twenty-three dollars and fifty cents." He looked at the photographs and began to ask me questions. These cabinets had been dreadful before, but now they were fine pieces. He ordered not only the combination, but also other styles of bookcases and player-roll cases from the photographs and lists I had made up.

When I got back to the Federal office, I opened up my salesbook and began counting the number of pieces. It added up to three hundred. One of the officers said, "What are you doing, Kahn?"

I said, "I'm writing up an order."

"For whom?"

"Hearn's. About three hundred pieces."

He couldn't believe that I had sold three hundred pieces to

them. He called the other salesmen over to take a look. I explained how I had gone out to Sheboygan and had pictures taken and had sold by the pictures.

That original Sheboygan shipment of two carloads of furniture to Hearn's went like the spring wind on Fourteenth Street. My status at Federal suddenly changed. My district was no longer limited to the Lower East Side. I went over to Macy's and told the buyer in the music department about my line of player-roll cabinets and piano benches. I asked for a test of ten samples. Macy's sold all of them off the floor in a day. They went up to twenty, thirty, and finally began buying in carloads that went up to ten carloads a week.

Through this period I consulted Judge regularly. He was moving with his wife and family to Virginia Beach in September 1925. However, I continued to get readings from him on every major step I took. There was one rule about these readings that I always kept in mind: The readings outlined the opportunity indicated by what Judge called "the forces." It was then up to the individual to make the opportunity work out.

If Cayce told me it would be thus and so, I knew that it would be so, but that I had to do my part. I had to know all the time that God was on my side because what I was doing was right in His sight. Cayce always insisted on that.

I had followed the readings into the furniture business. They had also indicated that my future lay in radios and music. Soon the opportunity presented itself to take a step in that direction. Up until this time radios had not been encased in cabinets of any kind. I sold a young man at an electrical company, E. B. Latham and Company, the idea of putting a radio set into a large stand-up cabinet. It was a new idea, and the young man jumped at it, talked it over with his associates, and wound up ordering a thousand cabinets. When he asked me the price per cabinet, I had no idea what was fair. I gave them a figure of forty-six dollars apiece. It was way overpriced, whatever the wood used, but I didn't know any better and neither did they.

Under the contract, they were responsible for the shipping. The cabinets arrived badly battered–with doors out of shape, legs that wobbled, and hinges broken, but since they were an electrical firm and not in the furniture business, they had no repair shops and no way of getting the cabinets repaired. Young Latham came to me and said, "Dave, I've just been made a partner in my father's firm and I've got those thousand cabinets and half of them are no good. I've made a terrible mistake."

I had to get the Latham people out of trouble. I went over to R. H. Macy's and asked one of the elevator operators how I got to the office of the owner. He told me that was Mr. Jesse Isidor Straus on the ninth floor.

I went up to the ninth floor, slipped past whoever should have been out in front of Mr. Straus' office, and knocked on the office door. A voice said, "Come in." I went in and there was Mr. Straus behind a large desk. I told him who I was and that I had a problem with five hundred cabinets that could easily be put into perfect condition and could hold five hundred Atwater Kent radios.

Mr. Straus said, "But you can't get five hundred Atwater Kent radios at once; we can only get ten a week."

I explained that since the Latham Company was in the electrical and radio business, they could get the five hundred Atwater Kent radios. "But," I added, "they've got five hundred cabinets they can't use and they're stretched outside their shop from one end of the street to the other."

Mr. Straus thought a minute and said, "Let me call in my radio buyer."

The radio buyer came in, looked at me and said, "Why, hello, Dave."

It was another of those coincidences. This was Macy's radio buyer, Bill Topping, who had been one of my pals when we were in officer-training camp at Fort Benjamin Harrison. Bill turned to Mr. Straus and said, "I wound up a lieutenant in the line—Dave wound up an aide to the general."

I explained to them both that E. B. Latham and Company had no way to fix those cabinets damaged en route. For Macy's it would be a minor job in their repair shops. I also suggested that since they could buy the cabinets through me at cost they could offer Atwater Kent radios in cabinets at a sale price.

That was how the first radio set sale in America was held—at Macy's, which even then refused to be undersold. A few days later Macy's had to go out and start picking up the other five hundred sets that Latham had sold to various jobbers, because the sale was such a success.

Latham also represented General Electric and a number of smaller companies. One of his customers, Joe Fried, was bringing out a new line of radios and needed twenty thousand cabinets. Latham suggested he talk to me. Fried already had a sample of the cabinet he wanted. It was a handsome design. He agreed to pay $19.95 apiece for those cabinets if my company could make them.

I told the people at Federal Furniture about the deal. However, they said they had decided to have nothing more to do with cabinets. There had been too much trouble with the deal with Latham, even though it had finally worked out to everybody's profit. Did they mind my doing something with this particular deal on my own? They said not at all. I went out to Rockford, Illinois, where there was a cabinet company run by a wonderful cabinetmaker named O. E. Landstrom. I told him about the cabinet, showed him the blueprint Fried had given me, asked him to study it and quote me a price. When I came back in a few hours, he still refused to quote a figure. Instead he asked, "What are you offering for this work to be done?"

Since I always thought of thirteen as a lucky number for me, I said, "Thirteen dollars."

He said, "I am sorry. We can't make it for less than thirteen dollars and thirty cents. I have figured it out to the last penny."

I already had an order for better than nineteen dollars each in my pocket. This meant that I could gross nearly 120,000 dollars and net enough profit to pay off all the debts in Kentucky.

Landstrom told me, "Look, I don't want any chiseling. I don't care what you get. But I want thirteen dollars and thirty cents for every cabinet. Not one penny less."

I assured him there would be no problem.

The deal went through and produced a tremendous profit. I wanted to do the right thing by Federal Furniture even though they had turned the whole idea down and told me I was on my own. I talked it over with my mother who said I ought to go in and give them a check for the whole amount. Or at least I should let them know exactly what happened and give them something very substantial. Well, I went to Federal Furniture and told Ben Lauterstein and Irving Isaacs precisely what had happened. Even so, I offered to give them a share of my profit. I said, "Irv, I think you and Ben at least ought to make enough for each of you to buy a car out of this." The way I remember it, Irv Isaacs bought himself a Rolls Royce, which he kept for the rest of his life, and Ben bought himself a custom-built Cadillac.

Now I had the money to pay off those debts. As long as they had remained unpaid, Mother refused to move away from Lexington. Many of them I had paid over the years, as I was able. But now I returned to Lexington and put an advertisement in the paper that anyone with claims against the name of Kahn should bring them to our banker or attorney and if they were shown to be our just obligations they would be paid at once.

All the debts were paid and Mother and the family moved to New York City.

It was understandably a tremendous emotional experience for my mother to come North. It was a breakup of so much that had been her life for more than thirty years. In a letter to Judge, addressed to "My dear Judge," she wrote: "David is doing fine and I hope to see you oftener in our New York home than I saw you in our Kentucky home. I do hate to give up the home. All the children are leaving me, and I can't live by myself, as my children are my life—God bless them. . . ."

She thanked him for the readings he had given her about going to New York and apologized for her writing: "I was ill last week, feel better again today. My arm is slowly improving. I hope, dear boy, that you will excuse my script as I am so very nervous. Thanking you for your reading. Hope this letter finds you in the best of health. Always, Mother Kahn. . . ."

Early in 1925 she closed up her beautiful home in Lexington, put her real estate in the hands of an agent, and she and the seven children journeyed to New York.

She mentions her arm in this letter. This was an injury caused as she tripped down the steps. I am certain that this injury was a cause of other physical disorders that were to lead ultimately to her death. I am certain, also, as she was, that her life span would have been briefer if it had not been for the readings Judge gave and continued to give until almost the last year of her life—which was to be some ten years later. Mother always maintained that Cayce had given her at least eight to ten years of life, enabling her to see her children married or engaged before she left this plane.

As for engagement and marriage in my own case, the wheel of romance had begun to turn after I came to New York. It had begun for me when I went into the Belasco Theater in New York on a lonely evening and saw for the first time a beautiful actress onstage whose last name happened to be the same as mine.

CHAPTER 8

Lucille

It is hard to know when beginnings really begin, especially if one has come to grasp the possibility that there have been previous times on this earth for the individual, as I was to do through Judge and the life readings—those readings that traced the path of a subject through previous existences in past times.

But the beginnings with Lucille did start long before New York—in Texas, in 1917, I had met a man in the Army who mentioned that he had a cousin, a young lady by the name of Lucille Kahn, who was a member of the Dreyfus family in Tulsa. The fact that we shared the same last name caught my attention. Later, through this same young man I met another cousin of Lucille Kahn—a charming blonde with whom I spent an evening dancing.

Shortly after that I was shipped overseas.

Not until years later, after I had come to New York to launch my business career, did I hear of Lucille again. A typical young newcomer to the city, strolling one evening through the theatrical district I passed by the Belasco Theater on West 44th Street, where a recently opened David Belasco production of a play called *Laugh, Clown, Laugh* was currently running.

Lonely, I went inside to see the show. Ian Keith and Lionel Barrymore were among the leading players. Among the characters in the story were a mother and daughter. The daughter was played by a girl with dark-brown hair, who appeared to be perhaps eighteen or nineteen years old.

I was impressed with her beauty. When the house lights went up I was able to look for the character in the program and found that the actress playing the part was—Lucille Kahn. The name rang a bell. I remembered my friend from Texas through whom I had heard of Miss Kahn. I also recalled that someone had written me that there was a Miss Kahn playing in a Broadway show.

Hurriedly I wrote a note asking if she was a part of the Dreyfus family of Tulsa, Oklahoma, and asked the usher to take the note backstage for me. The usher said, "Miss Kahn's only in the second act, sir. She's gone back to her hotel." He said this hotel was near the theater and he could take the message to her. Word came back from her that she was a member of the family in Tulsa and would I call her at ten-thirty in the morning? I did call in the morning and that night had dinner with her—and her sister, Alyce. I had a feeling that this beautiful Lucille, full of life, full of laughter, wanted me to date her sister. But charming as the sister was, it was Lucille I was falling in love with from the start.

We had many wonderful times in the months ahead. I told her, as I had told everyone else, about Cayce and how he guided me in my work. Near the end of the year of 1924 *Laugh, Clown, Laugh* went on the road. The following season, Lucille was given the coveted role playing opposite Otis Skinner in a production of *Sancho Panza*. The show went on tour, and Lucille was a hit in it. When it reached Tulsa, Oklahoma, she was greeted with such a triumphant welcome that Otis Skinner, not understanding the background, was somewhat miffed and declared that Lucille had "stolen the show."

Lucille had to explain that her family, which was quite a large clan, had lived there since—and as she paused, Skinner, accepting his fate, finished, "Since God was a boy." She laughed and nodded her head. Her family had been prominent in the community for many years, having come to this country from Alsace Lorraine. It wasn't surprising that when this young lady achieved such a success on Broadway, solely on her ability to play the role, the whole family and its large circle of friends wanted to turn out and cheer for one of their own.

During this period, I had not only told Lucille about Judge, I had told Judge about her. I had a feeling that for a long time both she and her sister thought of Cayce as "the funny man" who did all those incredible things that they really didn't wholly believe, even though Lucille found the stories interesting and delighted in relating them to others.

I suggested that when the company got to Dayton, Ohio, where Cayce had moved just prior to settling in Virginia Beach permanently, she call him and give him a chance to give her a reading.

Inwardly more serious about psychic matters than I at first realized, Lucille did call the Cayces and invited them to the show. They came to see the performance that night in early December 1924.

The meeting with the Cayce family in Dayton was a culmination of events that had begun with our first date—months before. But perhaps Lucille herself should tell this part of the story:

"Let me say that when I first met Dave I had a perspective slightly different from his about the whole thing. And about Dave. I did have a note from him because he had seen me in *Laugh, Clown, Laugh* and realized I was the Miss Kahn he was supposed to meet. And he did call the next morning as I suggested, and we did make a date for that night.

"That night, as it turned out, marked events destined to mold and shape my life in a direction hitherto unimaginable to me.

"After Alyce, Dave and I were seated at a table, Dave asked me to dance. As we seemingly floated across the floor—Dave was always a beautiful dancer—he asked me for my birth date and when I told him he proceeded to tell me all about myself. I thought, what a curious man. Of course, I knew nothing about horoscopes and had never even heard of pyschic phenomena or of a man named Edgar Cayce. So engrossed was I in hearing all about "me" that time became nonexistent. This kept on until finally I said, "You know, this is a continuous band and we have probably been dancing a terribly long time."

"When we returned to the table, my sister, quite unaccustomed to sitting alone in a night club, was in a huff. We apologized, explained about the band, and Dave asked her to dance. At first, she refused and then when he persisted she said, "Well, if in order to get home I must dance with you, let's get it over with!" They danced and danced and then I got angry. I was sure he was telling her all about *herself*. But he was really telling her about Edgar Cayce.

"When they finally came back to the table, Dave was still telling her—and now me—about Edgar Cayce, and Alyce kept nudging me under the table to indicate that she was simply not believing any of this nonsense. I didn't believe it either. But I did think it was vastly amusing and interesting. I told the cast the next day I had met a great raconteur whose repertoire included many strange tales. I was going to introduce him to them.

"On that first evening Dave made what I thought was his first error in credibility, as far as I was concerned. He told me about one of those coincidences that he said happened to him all the time. He told me that when he was stationed in Fort Worth he had taken a young girl by the name of Bernice Fox to her first officer's dance.

"Bernice happened to be my first cousin, and this supposedly had happened long before I came to New York to go on the stage. She came from Houston and was studying music in Fort Worth. I simply didn't believe him. I asked him what she looked like and he said she had long golden hair and was very charming. I simply wrote and asked Bernice if she knew him and she wrote back describing Dave exactly. It did make me begin to wonder about the many incidents Dave related to me which he was so sure were more than coincidence.

"I found him fascinating with his stories of business and all his deals in this new world of radio and cabinets—the first time anyone had ever put radio sets into beautiful cabinets which were themselves fine pieces of furniture. And all the stories about Mr. Cayce and how he guided Dave and how Dave would do nothing important until he telephoned or wired Cayce for a reading.

"When the play went on the road and we reached Dayton, Ohio, where Cayce and his family were then living, Dave told me I ought to get a reading. I agreed to call Cayce, and he and his family accepted my invitation to see the show. Afterwards they came backstage.

"It was very pleasant to meet them. I told them how much I'd heard about them. Then I said, 'Mr. Cayce, you've seen our show. Now I want to see yours.'

"Mr. Cayce told me I would have to get up early to see his show. I arrived at his home at 10 A.M. the next morning. It was my first time to witness and hear a reading. He went through what was to become for me the familiar ritual—unbuttoning his collar, leaning down to loosen his shoestrings, then loosening his trouser belt and stretching out on the studio-type couch he used because of his height. Then he closed his eyes and opened them again and you could see the blue eyes staring. Then, as the lids began to flicker, the suggestion was given.

"A young man was there that day, taking down the reading, and Gertrude was conducting.[1] The subject concerned a young child who could not keep any food down, and the parents, in desperation after exhausting all medical means, turned as a last resort to Cayce, whose psychic abilities in diagnosing physical ailments they had heard about. Following instructions, they wrote a letter telling him only that their child was in need of his help.

"Cayce in the reading declared that the child would recover if placed on a diet solely of ripe bananas. I had never heard anything like it before in my life. Here was a man who had attended grammar school for only a few years who was daring to prescribe a course of treatment for a desperately ill child.

"I was outraged. I thought this man ought to be put in jail for practicing medicine without a license. I was hoping the parents wouldn't be foolish enough to treat the child by feeding it ripe bananas on the suggestion of a man who had never even studied medicine.

"Still shocked by this, I followed up this case when I saw the Cayces on a later occasion and learned to my astonishment that the child was getting along very well.

"It was to be many years before medicine would catch up and begin to discover the many uses of ripe bananas in various diets and modern therapies.

"But even while I found it extremely difficult to accept such things I also found it engrossing and exciting. I did ask if I could have a reading. He gave me an appointment for another day."

[1] Cayce's secretary, Gladys Davis, who normally would have conducted, was attending her father's funeral in Alabama. This child's case is No. 4281 in the Cayce records.

Cayce could not give the reading for Lucille herself immediately but would later. There were many readings ahead from people all over the country, even then. Her show was playing in Indianapolis by the time he was able to give her reading. Gertrude was the conductor and there was a stenographer present to take notes.

"Yes, we have the body here," this reading on Lucille began. "Spiritually, and mentally and financially. Now we find all these exhibits of a physical body in a material world in this entity and very well balanced. There may be many conditions that bring improvements to the mental and financial from different standpoints, however, than from those at present expressed. . . .

"In the spiritual we find the entity one well awakened to the spiritual development for self and in and for others; one awakened sufficient to the necessity of spiritual forces entering in every physical and mental action. . . .

"Only keep that spiritual insight; only temper every physical action, every mental force, with that spiritual development that would bring the greater success to the entity, to the body in the material world and in the spiritual world beyond. . . .

"In the mental forces, we find one well adapted to the present conditions and endeavors; one capable of going much higher in the dramatic elements of the profession. . . .

"One whose physical and mental would lend their aid to such development and with spiritual insight the entity can and would carry a message to many peoples through such endeavors. . . .

"*Q.* Has this entity the necessary qualities to attain great heights in the drama?

"*A.* We have given it.

"*Q.* Could the entity make a success of her career if married to a businessman?

"*A.* In such relations, we find that there enters much that divides the mentalities of an entity attempting to give a message through its gifts or art, and in this we find the body no different from others in that a divided house gives not the best to the ones attempting to be benefitted, bringing then bad for all.

"*Q.* Would there be progress and contentment in her home if she renounced her career for marriage?

"*A.* The body, mentally and spiritually capable of renouncing career for another career, establishing and making a home, the greater career an individual can make in an earth's plane, for it becomes a pattern of that sort before the inmost of every entity. This individual must decide that for self. There are the possibilities, the qualifications, for the entity to make a success from either; not possible to make both.

"*Q.* How long should she remain on the road?

"*A.* Depending on decision of the entity as to what shall be made the career of the life's work.

"*Q.* Under whose management should she seek to advance her art?

"*A.* Not given from here. . . ."

On April 18, 1927, in a small family wedding in Ardmore, Oklahoma, Lucille Kahn and I were married.

Our honeymoon took us to Chicago and then east to Virginia Beach, where Cayce and his family had moved. I wanted Lucille to come to know the Cayces as intimate friends, as I had come to know them. I knew that they too would love her.

For in a sense in marrying me she was marrying also the Cayce family, and Judge himself, and the forces on which he drew and through which he was beginning to make his imprint on the world.

All of this would have to become as inseparable a part of Lucille's life as it was of mine.

CHAPTER 9

Sand and Sea

Virginia Beach—to which we were heading because I wanted her to have answers to all her own questions about Cayce and his work—was a strip of miles of magnificent beach front world. It was a place of ocean and skies, of tides and wind and surf roar.

It was to be the home not only of Judge and his family but of the whole Cayce story and its future. Yet those first years at the beach were not to be any placid sunset calm. Quite the opposite. It was a tumultuous, exciting, often turbulent period in all our lives, as unpredictable as the sea itself.

As the Cayce story unfolded and as Judge's work began to be more and more known, so also did the demands increase, the needs, challenges, conflicts, and the trials. The trials in fact—in a quite literal sense.

Much of this arose from the duality of Judge's nature, as I saw it. It was the things that he knew totally in trance but did not know at all in normal life, that he could foretell for others and could not foresee for himself. It was the psychic and human aspects swirling, seething, withdrawing again—like the seas at his doorstep.

Each aspect was both a part of the sea of Cayce's life, yet each was also a separate and individual story.

Lucille and Cayce liked each other. She had become interested in his work—and also somewhat alarmed. Some of it worried her. All the way to Virginia on one visit we made there later in the fall of 1927—we had been there briefly during our honeymoon in the spring—we talked about the situation. She was particularly disturbed that I actually guided myself in business by what Judge told me. Lucille pointed out that one of Cayce's most important statements to me, regarding a possible forthcoming merger of Federal with a number of other furniture companies, had not come into reality, although the date at which Cayce had said the merger would take place had already passed.

I told her to wait until we talked with Judge at his home in Virginia Beach. I did point out that Judge himself never turned away skeptics or investigators. He always told me and others that if anything he did or said was wrong, untruthful, or harmful—he wanted to be the first to know, and if it were proved to be so, he would give up the readings.

My relationship with Cayce was a fundamental part of my business and personal life, as Lucille had to understand. If I needed him, I called him. If he needed me, he called me. Many times I had emergency calls for financial help. Except for his photography, Cayce never had a business himself. Whatever the state of his finances, the readings were never commercialized. Cayce could not use them to help himself in the everyday matters of supporting himself and his family. The readings served to guide only others to health and happiness.

With his wife Gertrude, we set up a membership organization so that he could have some kind of drawing account on which to live, so that he would be protected in giving the readings, and so that the public that kept constantly increasing its demands on him would not overtax his strength. The readings warned that he should give only two readings a day, one in the morning and one in the afternoon. As long as we stayed with this limitation, Cayce continued with the work without ill effect. Years later, with the coming of World War II and the increasing demand for readings as a result of the casualties, he began to be importuned day and night. Believing it was his patriotic duty to play his part in the war, he was giving as many as five or six readings a day and sometimes more to meet the flood of wartime appeals. Demands of such proportions on Judge's physical strength became overwhelming.

Many times I have been asked "the truth" about my friend Judge. Did I ever suspect that what he did was fraud, deliberate or subconscious? Did I ever believe that he was drawing answers from clues given by those who came to get his readings or even receiving telepathic communication from the subject or others?

I can only say this: Before each reading Cayce was told only the name and address of the subject. He was not given, nor did he want, any further information. Many readings were given for people who had never met him or anyone associated with him. It is true that I arranged for readings for many people, some of whom I knew well, others only very casually. In these cases, it is possible that Cayce may have received some telepathic communication from me about the subjects. But even if that were true, what could he have learned from me? Perhaps he might have derived the general information that the person appeared to be well or ill, content or troubled, but not specific physiological details about which I was ignorant, and certainly not medical diagnoses of conditions and prescriptions for their treatment.

Most of Cayce's psychic life flowed through the readings, but there were other aspects that came when he was fully awake and aware of the incidents. His second son, Edgar Evans Cayce, for example, relates an incident, later mentioned in an article in *Fate* magazine: Cayce one day passed a woman as he was going up the stone steps to a post office. A warning came to him about this woman whom he didn't know. It impelled him to turn around and say to her, "Please—don't take any kind of auto ride today."

Insane as it must have seemed to her, she apparently realized that this tall man who spoke was obviously in earnest about the warning. The article by young Cayce declared, "That evening she rang our doorbell. She said she had been directed to our house from her description of Dad. Because of his warning she'd canceled a date to go riding with a friend that day. The friend had gone alone and had a serious accident. The woman was puzzled but grateful. . . ."

Judge lived by a timeless morality. He taught Sunday school, believed in Biblical truth, in human honesty in his fellow man. He wanted to harm nothing and no one. He carried his gifts as a sacred trust.

Yet, as late as the mid-1920s, Judge was still trying to find a way to keep on with his readings and somehow make a living to support his family properly.

One letter he wrote to me presents the picture. He refers in it to a reading he had given for a woman who had written to him through me:

"Mrs. L. had her reading, it is not a general reading and if it don't [sic] apply to her then it is a miss and the first one in 8500.

"But were I to take up any other work like the factory skeedoo for the other I am through for all times but I am going to have to do something unless can make some change, can't get along without eating and am having to try it these days, honest to God I am. . . .

"Anything Dave that you could find that I could make a

living for myself and family and that would give me a chance to work.

"Let me hear every chance Dave,

Ever the same,
Cayce"

I sent him funds at once, as I did regularly. So did many others who were helped by him. Voluntary gifts came, but they were never enough to do more than let him barely survive. There had to be a program set up so that he could carry on his work, without concern.

We had already begun to think about a membership organization, the dues of which could maintain Judge and his family. He would never be rich but we felt that he had a right to obtain enough for his needs—for some kind of stabilized program to support himself and his family.

It was shortly after that letter that the Cayces moved to Virginia Beach. The readings said that he should move to Virginia Beach because of the healthful conditions, the therapeutic values—particularly the iodine—in the sands, the proximity of New York and Washington, and because Cayce's own reading indicated that his future lay in this wild stretch of sand dunes and sea, at that time virtually undiscovered.

A part of the saga of Cayce and these sands centered about the Blumenthal brothers, and around my relationship with them and with Judge.

Because this story extends both before and beyond the October day in 1927 when Lucille and I were en route to Virginia Beach, and because of Morton Blumenthal's role in the unfolding Cayce saga, it is important to put this episode into perspective at this point.

I first met the Blumenthals, a family of financiers, in the early 1920s, through business associations in Altoona, Pennsylvania. Through them, I met Morton and Edwin Blumenthal in New York City. Morton and I became close friends. I knew that I needed someone with acumen and experience to assist me in carrying out the programs Judge and I had been considering. These included control over the readings and the strain put on Cayce; it included also plans for the hospital, a dream Cayce had never abandoned.

Morton was a true student in this field. He had read extensively the literature of psychic phenomena. Through me he obtained a number of readings which helped his family. Over the years during which he was associated with Cayce, he and his brother had many readings which helped to direct them in the accumulation of a sizable fortune. He gradually became more and more involved with Cayce's work and with plans to free Cayce from all strain of economic problems. After readings said that the sands of Virginia Beach were of special therapeutic value (especially for sand baths with the body covered in the sand from the feet to the neck), the Blumenthals put up funds that made possible the purchase of the property at Virginia Beach.

Judge gave many readings for the Blumenthals and also for their friends and associates. One unusual case concerned a friend of Morton whose young daughter, according to the doctors, was close to death. Since medicine had apparently given up, the man was glad for any glimmer of hope. In the reading, Cayce advised that a certain preparation be given as the way to save the child's life. When the father took the prescription given by Cayce to the druggist, the pharmacist refused to fill it. The father, with no other hope in sight, went behind the counter himself, filled the prescription, and administered it to the child. The child recovered, grew up to be a perfectly healthy individual, and by the 1960s not only had children, but grandchildren of her own.

Morton Blumenthal and I had many discussions about procedures. We could not charge fees and did not want to. However, we could not depend on voluntary gifts alone. Promises to give were not always fulfilled. Persons who came for readings in serious cases, often after the doctors had given up entirely, would promise anything to get help. But then if help came and they found themselves well, the doctors who had given up earlier would often tell them that they would have gotten well anyway.

In 1927, we finally formed the Association of National Investigators, chartered for the purpose of psychic research. To get a reading, a person had to join the association. Membership cost ten dollars. Out of membership fees Judge and his family could be maintained with some kind of income, not any great sum, but sufficient to meet essentials without nagging need.

Morton had purchased the property for Judge at Virginia Beach in 1924. In November 1927, we completed the building which was to be the hospital. All of us contributed to this effort in work, in funds, in whatever ways we could.

The Blumenthals contributed most of the funds that were needed and continued to give a part of their income to the association. Morton gave at least half of his time to work for the association and for Cayce.

Judge's own family were helping, including Gertrude, the boys, his older sister Annie. The warm and always gracious Gladys Davis, his secretary, worked tirelessly with us. My family also gave in whatever way we could, and as one of our contributions, we provided the furnishings for the hospital except for the medical equipment. The board of the association consisted of Morton and Edwin Blumenthal, Hugh Lynn Cayce, myself, and other associates, business and financial advisers.

There were eventually three buildings—a nursing home, the Cayce home, and the main building, which we called the hospital.

The hospital soon became a going operation, but it was never really self-supporting because of poor management and too many charity patients. Judge's readings on "the work" kept insisting that a superintendent for the hospital be secured. This was not done.

We did have an excellent licensed medical staff and nurses, however. Cayce's readings formed the basis of the medical program and treatment for the patients.

Among Morton Blumenthal's contributions to the cause at Virginia Beach was the formation of Atlantic university. He felt that the university could be an important part in the unfolding of Cayce's work. Judge personally was not too keen on this development because he was afraid it would interfere with the work at the hospital, which had always been his primary concern.

But the university plan plunged ahead with Morton providing funds to bring together a staff. A distinguished psychologist, who had been one of Hugh Lynn's professors at Washington and Lee University, Dr. William Moseley Brown, was made president of the university. Dr. Brown brought together an outstanding faculty and a sizable student body—even before lecture hall buildings were completed. The first year started with high hopes in two ocean-front hotels rented for the school months. Unfortunately, even with the best will in the world, questions of control and authority arose, particularly as we reached the 1929 financial crash and the depression that followed.

The question of who should determine and direct what was to be done reached a climactic point when Morton Blumenthal suggested that in the future, when Cayce desired to give a reading for anyone other than a health reading, he would first have to clear it with him.

I learned about this at a meeting at Virginia Beach at which I happened to be present. Cayce turned to Morton and said, "As much affection as I have for you and as much as I appreciate all you have done for me, on the day that I cannot give a reading for David E. Kahn or any member of his family or anyone he suggests—on that day 'little Eddie' will be six feet under the ground."

He said this very deliberately, and he pointed to himself as he said it.

He bent down and picked up his cap and coat. He said, "I am through and you can take it."

Then came the slow erosion of funds as the rift widened. It reached the point where there were no more funds. The university had to close before the end of the second year; the Association of National Investigators was dissolved; the patients in the hospital were told to leave; the building would close its doors. All of this took place under Morton's direction. The whole endeavor dissolved. Morton Blumenthal died, and the buildings were finally sold off for taxes. Cayce and his family had to give up even the home which had been bought for them but had not legally been put in their name. They moved into a rented house, and all of us pitched in and helped refurbish it to make it livable for Judge, Gertrude, and the boys.

It was then, in March 1936, that we decided to reorganize our activities under the name of the Association for Research and Enlightenment, Inc., an organization that has grown in stature and meaning across America over the decades since that time. The name was suggested in a reading.

Ultimately also, the people of Virginia Beach came to love, even revere, Edgar Cayce and his family. In time the new association was able to buy back the buildings and in March 1956 began to remodel and rebuild.

I have interrupted the chronology to tell the Morton Blumenthal story here because of the parallel of our own involvement—Lucille's and mine—over the same years. In much of it we would be directly involved. But we had also our own personal lives and our own relationship with the Cayces. This was the world to which I was bringing Lucille in the fall of 1927—when she was so concerned about the business readings Cayce was giving me and the fact that he had predicted a major merger in the furniture business that seemingly had not occurred.

The reading given to me in the spring of the year I was married stated that the Federal Furniture factories, Irving Furniture, Federal Metal Beds Company, and other associations owned by my firm would merge with a very large national company in October 1927.

It said that because of the work I had done, I would be made a vice-president of the new company, a position of considerable importance in the furniture business. I was at that time operating as vice-president of individual companies and was still actively running the Sheboygan plant.

Lucille was her gracious self when we arrived on that visit to Judge and the family. I knew that she was doing her very best to accept all these things. I knew that she wanted my success. But she did not want my future to be threatened, as she saw it, by my complete reliance on what Judge might say in the readings.

After we had been there a little while, Lucille said to Cayce, very gently but firmly, too, "Judge, I want you to do me a favor. Please stop giving Dave business readings."

I remember the look Judge gave her—a curious look, as though he could not quite believe what he had heard. Lucille went on, "You gave Dave a reading about a merger that would take place in October and it hasn't happened. He's been depending upon it and telling people about it, and it just isn't right."

Then she quickly added, "You give wonderful readings on mental, spiritual, and physical problems. But stay away from the business things. It's not for you." There are moments when Lucille can be quite positive and determined.

Judge didn't hesitate an instant. "As long as he wants a reading," he asserted, "I don't ask him what it's about. He can get a reading as often as he wants and when he wants it."

They were looking at each other there in the room. And Judge went on very slowly. "But if I ever give one that's harmful, that hurts him, I'll never give another one for anybody." Then, with a change of tone that was one of his surprising characteristics, he said, "Let's go back and see what we get."

We all went back to his little room and he took off his tie and unbuttoned his collar as usual and lay on his back, hands on his stomach, and gazed up at the ceiling. I made the suggestion to him, just as the lids were closing, "Now, Mr. Cayce, you're going to sleep. You'll hear me and you'll give the information now. This is in reference to a prophecy you made some time ago that there would be a merger—"

Before I could finish this sentence he interrupted me with, "That's going to be made. What's your hurry?"

I said, "It hasn't happened yet and we'd like to know why."

I went on to complete my suggestion then and he went on with the reading. He said that the merger was set but had not yet been completed, that it would be completed early in November.

He said that there would be many lines of manufactured articles involved and they would be sold all over the country. When I tried to pin him down about these, the "forces," as Cayce called them, became very sharp, and told me to wait and see. I would know in due season. But the merger—it was reaffirmed positively—would happen.

In my office on Lexington Avenue in New York City, the following afternoon, I found a group of leading furniture people gathered in consultation. There were top people from Bloomingdale's, the head man at Spear's furniture store, the heads of a number of other major retail furniture outlets. They were discussing this great merger which they had apparently learned had already taken place.

I told all these people, who would be among our chief customers when the deal went through, that the merger had not been signed. I said it would happen but had not happened yet. This was based on Judge's reading of the day before.

That evening, I drove uptown with Mr. Isaacs of Federal Furniture. On the way he told me that clients of Manufacturer's Trust, one of the country's great banks, owned a number of furniture plants but that they were getting out of direct operation of commercial business and wanted us to take over all these furniture plants. Acquisition of these plants would make us the largest manufacturer of hotel supplies and furniture in the nation.

"But you still haven't signed the agreement," I said.

He said, "How would you know?"

"I've been to Virginia Beach."

Isaacs made a grimace and said, "Are you still fooling around with that crazy guy?"

I said, "He's not so crazy. If it hadn't been for him, I would have accepted a job with another firm two weeks ago. Cayce told me to stick with you, that my future was with you. So if you value me at all you should be thankful for Edgar Cayce. Besides, you have a relative who's been ill and is getting well right now at Virginia Beach."

"I'm not criticizing your Cayce," he said. "But it just seems strange that a huge business is run on a psychic's advice."

I said, "Well, we don't have to go into that now. But I do know the results. Cayce said I would work in wood and metal. I'm only here a short time and we're making products of wood and metal, and we're doing very well."

He smiled. He couldn't argue with that statement.

As close as I can remember, it was on November 10 that

the merger was finally signed. It brought together eighteen plants under a corporate umbrella known as Albert Pick-Barth and Company. I was in charge of the entire furniture end of the operation. This included more than a half dozen plants in various parts of the nation, including Federal's very successful plant in Asheville, North Carolina, which I was eventually to run personally.

The merger, of which Cayce had been so positive, created a new major corporation.

CHAPTER 10

"To Know . . . Ask!"

The forces did not volunteer information. You had to ask the questions. It was as if Judge drew upon some unplumbed sea where all knowledge, all time, all meaning resided, and all answers could be had. The reading would give generalized information, but for more detailed data, questions to which that data applied had to be asked.

I relied on his answers as I would on the answers of my own lawyer or doctor. Even more. Yet in retrospect I realized that there were times when the right questions were not asked.

The story of Cayce, myself, and the Paris Medicine Company is a twenty-five-million-dollar case in point.

In the first years of my career in furniture and cabinets I had done extremely well. I had gained a reputation as the first to put radios into cabinets that were beautiful pieces of furniture. From there—always with Cayce in the background guiding each major step—I pushed ahead.

Fate spins a slender thread in some of these matters. Guided by a Cayce reading, I took some of the executives of General Electric down to Asheville, North Carolina, to see the Carolina Wood Products plant which I was operating there for our company, Albert Pick-Barth. We were discussing with them a large order for cabinets. The Asheville plant was turning out a flood of radio cabinets for the expanding market. In fact, the cabinets ultimately pushed the furniture business right out of that Asheville plant. The General Electric people made a number of trips down there. On several of these trips Lucille went with me. We stayed at the Grove Park Inn, one of the most beautiful hotels in the world, which was owned by Fred Seely.

A warm relationship developed between Seely and myself, and between our families. In that beautiful inn with its huge fireplace and its handsome furnishings and grounds, we spent many evenings with the Seelys. When Lucille was expecting our first child, Seely's daughter was in China also expecting her first child—they were actually born three days apart. When we were in Asheville in those days, Mrs. Seely would take Lucille in her arms and hold her close as if Lucille were her daughter, too.

It was through Fred Seely that the somewhat incredible Paris Medicine story developed.

Paris Medicine was the company that made E. W. Grove's Bromo-Laxative-Quinine. People all over the world bought this cure for colds, headaches, and other minor ailments. Seely and his brother-in-law, Edwin Grove, owned the company. Seely wanted to sell it, but he could not do so unless his brother-in-law, who held the controlling interest, agreed to sell as well.

Seely decided that I was the one man who might be able to convince his brother-in-law that the sale would be advantageous to both of them. "Dave," he said, "you can talk him into it. I'll back you up and I'll get you all the figures. The bank—they're the executors of the estate of Mr. Grove—will agree because we'll have all the proper information."

I was aware that we were not talking about a simple business deal. It was a transaction that would involve many people, many factors of timing and circumstances, and an extremely large amount of money. I said, "The only way I could possibly do this is to talk to Cayce and have him talk to you and get all the information about it. The only thing I'd suggest is that I get Mr. Cayce to come down here and give us a reading."

He wanted to know how we did this. I said, "If you call him and tell him you'll pay his expenses down here and put him up at the inn, he'll come, and if he tells me I can do this for you, or should try to do it, well—then I'll do it."

Mr. Seely said, "You've got yourself a deal." He put in a call for Judge, told him that we needed his guidance and asked him to come down. I warned Seely we were not to give Cayce any information about the problem itself beyond Seely's name and the address.

Judge arrived the following day and, after some discussion and a tour of the inn and the grounds, took off his shoes and stretched out on the bed, hands on his abdomen, his eyes looking up at the ceiling. I gave him the usual directions and he went into trance.

The reading said that there would be a deal. It said that I should leave in December and go to see Mr. Edwin Grove. The reading declared that I would probably be received without very much enthusiasm by Mr. Grove, who would indicate that he was not very much interested in the project or me. The reading went on to say that I was not to take this to heart and that if I persevered, it would work out; I was just to remember that I would be seeing him in April following the first meeting and that a deal would be made.

The following December I went to St. Louis. Acting on instructions from Seely, the chairman of the board of the St. Louis Union Trust Bank gave me the figures on the last ten years of the Paris Medicine Company. I told the chairman, Isaac M. Orr, that I wanted so see Mr. Edwin Grove.

Mr. Orr said he didn't think Mr. Grove would see me; he had turned down many previous offers and did not like to be bothered with these overtures. "But, since Mr. Seely is interested in this," he said, "it's up to you. I'll do what I can."

Mr. Orr also told me that the price of the business, if it ever were sold, would be approximately eleven million dollars.

I met Mr. Grove in his lawyer's office. A toothless, paunchy, heavy-set man, he hardly looked like the usual multimillionaire. I decided not to approach the subject head on. But before I could speak he said, "Mr. Kahn, you are the forty-sixth feller who's been out here to see me. The business is not for sale."

I countered that I wasn't there to buy his business. I said I didn't care how many bankers had come there trying to buy his company. "I don't blame you for turning them down," I said. "I think you're one of the best merchants I ever met. If the tables were turned, I'd do the same thing you're doing—I'd keep it."

The faintest of smiles came to his lips. "I'm glad there's one sensible guy who realizes what we've got," he told me. "It's not up for sale. There's no use even talking."

"Yes," I said, "and I just wanted to come and talk to you. I'm vice-president of Albert Pick-Barth of New York and we have some big customers here in St. Louis. . . ."

I plunged on, giving him the general sales talk as fast as I could, letting him know he wasn't talking now to a banker but to a merchandiser like himself. I said, "Mr. Grove, if somebody offered me fifteen million dollars I think I'd take it. . . ."

And he sort of looked at me hard and said, "If somebody offered me fifteen million, I would take it. The damn company bothers me."

Mr. Grove told me he was going on a yachting trip. I told him I'd see him when he got back—on April 13, my lucky day. When I did see him—on April 13—he said, "Kahn, you don't take no for an answer."

"You didn't say no," I countered. "You said maybe."

I was counting on a gambit. He had fifteen million dollars now in his mind. I was counting on the fact that he and his brother-in-law, Seely, did not agree on how to run the business. The bank would get eleven million as trustees and this money would be divided between Edwin Grove and Seely according to the number of shares each held. An additional four million would go to Grove with everybody's knowledge, in order to make Grove feel he was getting rewarded for his role in building up the company. And I would make a considerable sum as my commission.

Grove liked me and he liked the deal. He took me out to a ball game in St. Louis, and he took me out to meet his family. He also gave me ten years of the records of the Paris Medicine Company as audited by Price Waterhouse. Seely was delighted with the whole arrangement.

In the meantime, I started the search for a buyer. We made a tentative agreement with one company. It seemed set, but readings from Cayce told me that I would be released from this deal. Then we had another bid. Drugs Incorporated was willing to pay our price immediately. When I asked the first company what they wanted to do, it turned out that they in fact did want to be released, just as Cayce had said.

We now had a firm commitment that was ready to be put into effect immediately, and I and several others went to Boston where Mr. Grove was relaxing on his yacht.

He began to talk about the deal. Mr. Grove said to the others, "You know, Mr. Kahn here has been representing me one hundred per cent in this deal."

He took a piece of paper out of his pocket. It had some scribbled figures on it. He said, "But you know I've had a heart attack."

I didn't know where he was heading. Still looking at the figures, Grove went on, "We didn't add anything to the price to include in this sale the cafeteria my father established for the employees of Paris Medicine. When it started it was way out in the country, now it's in the middle of the city. We don't need the cafeteria, but we should be paid ten times the earnings we've earned on it plus the value of the land. So the price for the whole deal now becomes twenty-five million dollars."

I thought all the others were about to drop dead. It was just like that—an absolutely unlooked for ten million-dollar jump in the price. The others just shook their heads.

The deal appeared to be wrecked. But I had put a lot into it. And Cayce's reading indicated as they had all along that we *would* make a deal. I remembered that once in France during the war I'd gotten a good dinner of steak and biscuits for a visiting honorary general and his men. The general was Sam McRoberts, vice-president of the First National Bank of New York. Over the years he'd risen to be chairman of the board of the Chatham-Phoenix Bank. I called him, reintroduced myself, and had him call me while I was at Fred Seely's office in Asheville so that we could arrange a luncheon date in New York. During that luncheon, I brought up the Paris Medicine story.

McRoberts was startled. He said he had clients who had wanted to buy that company for years and had been trying desperately just to get the figures. I thereupon produced the Price Waterhouse figures I had obtained in St. Louis. McRoberts was really impressed. He wanted to know the selling price. I told him it was twenty-five million dollars.

McRoberts and the bank were working with the Zonite Company, who were the would-be buyers. The following day we worked out the details with the Zonite Company, and the papers were signed in St. Louis on October 10. The year was 1929.

The deal was completed; the commitment was irrevocable, the facts unquestioned; and Grove had the money. But then the stock market broke, and Grove came to me and said he would have to cut my commission in half. He handed me a paper signed by himself and Mr. Orr of the bank that I was supposed to sign, agreeing to the cut. I was so outraged at this treatment that I crumpled the paper and threw it in the trash.

After talking to Seely, I realized this paper could be valuable. I rushed back to the room where we had been talking and recovered the piece of paper Grove had handed me. I put it away with a feeling that perhaps someday it would be useful, particularly if I decided to take legal action.

Fred Seely asked me not to sue Grove right away but said that when things straightened out a little, he would be a witness for me. I went along with this. Judge in the readings told me to remember my promises to Fred Seely.

But only a little later Mr. Grove died. Under St. Louis law, if a man dies there's virtually no suit against his estate unless there are outside witnesses and evidence of the claims. What the dead man may have said to me was not admissible. But I did have that slip of paper. And eventually—when I took legal action—that paper was a key factor.

When I brought it in, it was a surprise to many people. I took the stand. I said, "Your honor, yesterday you said my lips were sealed unless somebody was involved in this deal besides Mr. Grove. Now I don't want to take any liberties with the court but may I show you this letter?"

I showed it to him and he asked counsel on both sides to come up to the bench and he showed it to them. And he asked, "Whose initials are these?"

I told him they were the initials of an officer of the St. Louis Union Trust, with whom I had talked and corresponded. The officer was put on the stand. He was seventy-seven years old and he had to look very closely through his thick-rimmed glasses to recognize the initials as his own. It was clear from this letter that they had agreed to my commission, even though they wanted to cut it.

This was enough to give me legal grounds to sue—the fact that it was not only Grove's signature, but also the initials of someone at the bank.

When the verdict came in, I found that the jury had accepted my claim that I was entitled to the commission. But they awarded me a sum considerably less than what was owed me. The judge sent for me and told me that only one man on the jury had held out for the low figure, even though the others felt I deserved the full amount. He said, "That's the way these things go, and there's often nothing to do except to accept it."

Cayce had said from the beginning that it would be a deal, and his readings had told me how to go about making these arrangements. But the readings had not mentioned one detail: that I would run into difficulty collecting my commission. I had it; it was a deal. It was a problem of collection.

Was it Cayce's error—or mine? On reflection, it occurred to me that it was not Cayce's error at all. It was always true that we had to ask, I had to ask, the proper questions. It was my impatience—my failure to seek guidance all the way through the deal. If I had taken the reduced amount Grove had offered me after the deal was closed, I would have walked away with much more than the jury awarded me. But this information could only have been available if I had taken time to ask.

In the matter of knowing what question to ask—or what lay directly ahead—even Judge himself was no different from the rest of us, except when in trance.

Twice in their lives the Cayces were brought into court, once in New York and once in Detroit, on assorted charges of telling fortunes or practicing medicine illegally. In both cases Cayce gave readings, indicating that the case was being carried properly and would come out in their favor. In the Detroit case, charges were dismissed except one technical charge to which a member of the Cayce party agreed to plea guilty; following a probational department report this was disposed of quickly without a fine.

The New York case received wide publicity, photographs and headlines in the papers. The facts were simple: Two women living in the hotel where the Cayces were staying in New York applied for readings. When a reading was given, they announced they were policewomen; detectives waiting in the hall came in and Cayce, Gertrude, and Gladys Davis were all placed under arrest.

The Cayces were found innocent of any legal violations—but legalities were not the true issue. The issue was the character of our Association for Research and Enlightenment and of Cayce himself.

Testifying for the defense, I told about the association, its work, its purposes. The district attorney asked about the formation of the organization. A fragment of this part of the trial reads as follows:

Q. What is it, spiritualistic?

A. No sir, it is just what the charter says. It is an organization that was organized for the investigation of this man's work. The man has an unusual—

Q. This defendant Cayce?

A. This man Cayce has an unusual power. What it is, no one has been able to tell. I have had lawyers, doctors, presidents of universities in this city, the most prominent people, and not any man has been able to say anything but that it is perfectly remarkable and what he says is the truth. We are investigating to see whether the things work out from the advice and counsel that he gives. That is what the association is organized for. We publish records. We meet regularly. We have various people coming from various places . . . to tell us what they think of it. I have known the man for almost thirty years, I've had him in more than twenty cities, not as a money-making proposition. . . . Our charter is organized for the purpose of investigation and these records are kept in our archives. We have an association for that purpose.

When Cayce was called to the witness stand, the judge on the bench asked the opening questions:

Q. You claim that you are a psychic?
A. No sir, I make no claims whatever. May I tell my story?
Q. Yes. I would like to hear it.
A. For thirty-one years I have been called or told that I was a psychic. It first began as a child. I didn't know what it was. When many people who had asked me to do things for them asked for advice and counsel, after it had gone on for years, it was investigated by individuals.
Q. And then the company was formed?
A. This company was formed to study the work.
Q. And they pay you a salary?
A. They pay me a salary.
Q. Do you go into a trance?
A. I do not know. I am unconscious.
Q. You are unconscious?
A. Unconscious. It has been called by some scientists, it has been investigated, it has been called, some call it hypnotic influence, some call it a trance.

After the district attorney cross-examined Cayce briefly the Court declared:

"Step down. Put this on the record. After seeing the People's witnesses and the three defendants and their witness on the stand, and observing their manner of testifying, and after reading the exhibits in the case, I find as a fact that Mr. Cayce and his co-defendants were not pretending to tell fortunes and that to hold these defendants guilty of a violation of Section 899 of the Code of Criminal Procedure, Sub-division 3, would be an interference with the belief, practices, or usages of an incorporated ecclesiastical governing body, or the duly licensed teachers thereof, and they are discharged. . . ."

After word had reached Virginia Beach of the arrest of the Cayces and Gladys—before the actual trial was held—Hugh Lynn wrote a letter in which he stated, among other comments:

"The morning papers explain your delay in detail. I entirely forgive you making me wait three hours at the train the other morning. Please let me know if you are comfortable in the present surroundings. I do hope they gave you a nice cell with plenty of light, running water, and whatnot. . . . Be sure and save me all the printed details in the papers there. It is quite thrilling to have parents in the papers, especially in jail. . . .

"Seriously . . . many people have been treated this way before you know from 10,500 B.C. to now. . . . The world is not kind to people who are different. Keep smiling and remember 'Father forgive them they know not what they do. . . .'"

This was before the outcome of the case was known.

But the question must be asked: Why didn't the reading reveal that these women were actually deceiving Cayce?

It may well be that when the situation concerns a deliberate deception of the psychic forces themselves, this could distort the forces or force fields and make them ineffective and inoperable.

In such a case there would be no correct answer. Or question.

CHAPTER 11

The Doors of Time

We became caught up in ourselves and in our own desires. I was not better or worse in this regard than others who listened to the Cayce readings but who did not always act on their implications. Approximately three months before the 1929 crash of the stock market, when everyone was involved in skyrocketing figures, Cayce warned me in a reading that the crash was going to come and advised that I get out of the market before this happened.

I did not doubt the reading. I did question the timing. Everything seemed to be going well. I had enough money to care for my mother, to help my brothers and sisters establish comfortable lives for themselves, and to provide for my wife and child. Actually, I didn't follow the market closely—it was the excitement of my business activities that concerned me. So I left my investments in the hands of brokers. Using my limited human range of knowledge instead of the sources on which Cayce drew, I had decided to wait and see. Like millions of others, I held on, and when the first weeks of the crash were over, I found that I had almost nothing left.

It was a rough blow and a tough period for all of us. We

still continued in our work with Virginia Beach, but often they, too, had a rough go of it. Some of my property holdings were still viable, including the plant in Asheville, over which I now had virtually complete control. The plant had survived the collapse of Albert Pick-Barth, which had been one of the largest furniture holding companies in the country, but which had not been able to withstand that economic cataclysm.

Other undertakings, where I heeded what Judge said in the readings, worked out magnificently. For example, during this period of the depression and the New Deal which followed, Cayce was giving me guidelines in regard to new roles I should play in regard to the government in Washington.

President Roosevelt had come into office; the banks had been closed for reorganization, and although bread lines and soup kitchens were still very much in evidence, there was a real sense of awakening forces and help in which I felt I should take part.

In one of the readings, Cayce informed me that I should write to Mrs. Roosevelt and ask if I could be of help to the country. He mentioned a specific project, which I had never heard about before the reading. The project was Arthurdale, a community in what is now called Appalachia, that long stretch of poverty and shacks and hunger along the main ridge of the Appalachian Mountains in the eastern United States.

Arthurdale, West Virginia, was named after a family there that owned a sizable farm. Mrs. Roosevelt and later Secretary of the Treasury Henry Morgenthau helped out in this community, where a scattered population of some two hundred coal-mining families existed on the brink of starvation.

As a pilot project developed partially by the government and partially by private interests, thirteen hundred acres of the farm land had been transformed into a complete model community. They had built homes, a chicken farm, a dairy farm, a grocery store, an inn, even a small hospital. They had also built factories through which they hoped to get an avenue not of charity but of work for the people. But the factories had failed.

I knew nothing about the Arthurdale story but it was there in the reading, so I wrote to Mrs. Roosevelt, told her I was particularly concerned with the situation I understood existed at Arthurdale, and asked what I could do.

I directed my letter to Hyde Park but as Mrs. Roosevelt was traveling all over the nation in those days, her answering letter came from Seattle, Washington. She asked me to meet her on the following Saturday at Hyde Park.

She was charming, gracious, and quite to the point about what was needed. I was a successful businessman and perhaps I could help. The people needed work, something to manufacture in the factories, something that would bring in outside money for them and their products.

I told her I had extensive operations in radio cabinets and that it might be possible that I could shift some of the production to Arthurdale. She asked me if I would go down there, look the whole property over, and, after examining the site and the problems involved, make recommendations.

Arthurdale had been greatly helped but remained, like so many other areas of America in that era, desperately in need of a real shot in the arm, in need of work, production, machinery. There was, however, machinery available and more could be brought in. Radio cabinets represented a product that could be of importance to the people of this community and of other communities, if it worked out.

I so recommended to Mrs. Roosevelt. The result was that we moved the entire production of cabinets from Celina, Ohio, to Arthurdale. This provided work and training programs for most of the men of that community and thereby provided funds for these people to buy food and clothes and maintain a reasonable standard of living.

It was a partnership in humanity, a combined operation of business, government, and individuals. We continued with this Arthurdale program for two years, by which time the people of the community had taken hold of their own destinies. During this same period I suggested to Mrs. Roosevelt that we develop a plan by which the people could buy their own homes, paying for them over the years on long-term work-credit basis.

Arthurdale put community effort and cooperation on a business basis. Other communities like this were developed in other parts of the nation. Many, I am told, are still thriving communities that go back, in their beginning, to those days of trial and testing.

Again, it was Cayce's reading that gave us the clue in a name neither he nor I had heard before—Arthurdale.

The interweaving threads of our lives still continued to develop, despite the depression. No major steps were taken without Cayce's advice. Lucille and I lived for a time in New York City and eventually made a home in Scarsdale. Judge would come there for a month at least twice a year and we would bring many people to meet him. By this time the world was beginning to hear about the work of this miracle worker of Virginia Beach. Many of our friends wanted to meet him; many wanted readings. The rule was that they could have readings only if they joined the Association for Research and Enlightenment, Inc.

Sometimes I would hold meetings at various centers or hotel meeting rooms in the city where I or others of the movement would talk about Cayce's work, and sometimes Cayce himself would be present at these gatherings. At these meetings I would tell some of the stories or experiences of other individuals who had been helped or cured through Cayce.

Some of these cases involved Cayce's remarkable ability to tap the channels of past or present in the readings—particularly in the life readings which he had started late in 1923 and in which he described previous incarnations of the individual. (This, it should be noted, was many years before the Bridey Murphy story and other experiments with hypnotic regression back to previous life experiences.) Yet there were other surprises—an episode could have its roots in a past-life experience or in the background of the present.

One case in point I recall citing from the platform at a rather large meeting concerned a man who had gone suddenly berserk. A man usually of kindness and gentleness, he was a relative of an employee in our home. As I related at the meeting—not identifying the man in any way—he had struck his wife and then his daughter. Alarmed relatives took him to New York's Bellevue Hospital. He was examined by psychiatrists, given a series of tests, and committed to Rockland State Hospital.

It was then, I told the audience, that the relative who worked in our home asked me if I thought Mr. Cayce could help. I telephoned Virginia Beach and asked Judge for a reading on this man. The only reference I gave him was the address and the name.

Cayce's reading said that the man had fallen on the ice some time ago and had injured himself. The reading said that the man needed not psychiatric but osteopathic treatment. We were able to have the man treated by an osteopath to whom the Cayce readings had sent other patients, Dr. Frank P. Dobbins. Later, when I spoke with the patient, he asked, "Mr. Kahn, do I look like a crazy man?"

I told him that in my opinion he was not crazy. I explained about the Cayce reading and the fact that it said specifically he had been injured in a fall on the ice. He shook his head in perplexity. How could this man named Cayce, whom he had never met or heard of, know such a trivial incident as the fact that he had fallen on the ice in December, three years past?

I did not tell any of this to Dr. Dobbins. I had put the reading, as they gave it to us from Virginia Beach, in a sealed envelope. The doctor made his examination and then opened the envelope. As he read the Cayce report, he kept saying, "This is very, very remarkable." He accepted the diagnosis as correct but did not want to treat the man precisely as Cayce's reading indicated. He stated, however, that it could do no harm. Further, nothing he had seen in the reading could have harmed a patient, and many things could be, and were, helpful. So he agreed to go ahead with Cayce's suggested treatment. Three months later the man was well.

In reporting this story to the large meeting in New York, I referred to the patient only as Mr. X. When I had finished, a tall, distinguished-looking man rose in the back of the auditorium and cried out, "Mr. Chairman, you're talking about me when you tell that story. I am your Mr. X."

He proceeded then to affirm to the audience the case in detail, step by step.

The depression had affected everyone, and business was extremely difficult. Although I held on personally to the Carolina Wood Products plant, the bankers thought I was in distress and would give it over to meet claims of creditors. But I told them they didn't have a chance of getting that plant because we had bought everything on consignment, all the glue and wood and everything; what we used and sold we paid for. The plant had contracted for some materials and the only way we could pay those bills was to separate our assets from the assets of the Albert Pick-Barth company. This we did.

In those dollar-bleak years every deal and every penny was a struggle. I was still in the furniture business but was gradually edging out. Judge would send me letters and readings. A number of readings said that for the time being I should get into the metal end of the business rather than the wood. I took on an order of thirty thousand metal cabinets for refrigerators but that deal lapsed, and after I had purchased the cabinets I had to find a buyer for thirty thousand refrigerator cabinets or take a big loss.

Judge gave me a reading which sent me to the right industrialist in Detroit and I was able to get rid of the refrigerator cabinets with a commission of nearly fifty thousand dollars.

In the wallowing seas of America's worst depression I was still afloat.

One of Judge's most important readings for me came during this period: He told me that I should buy the Brunswick Company, makers of radios and record-playing machines and records. I knew very little about Brunswick Radio except that it was a large and reputable company, yet here, all of a sudden, was Cayce telling me to buy it.

Talking motion pictures were just coming in and the movie people were buying into the sound-reproduction and record-making business. I contacted a man I had come to know because he came to our Cayce meetings in New York—motion picture producer Harry Goetz—and told him Cayce had said I should buy the Brunswick Company and that I would become the leading maker of radio cabinets in the country. Warner Brothers, with whom Goetz had close associations, had purchased the Brunswick Balke-Collander Company of Chicago for twenty-two million dollars. They then invested more in the company to develop the Brunswick Panatrope, one of the finest record players ever made, but they were losing too much on it because of the depression and had decided to sell off the electronic part of the business—a small part of the overall operation. Not even Harry Goetz, however, had known that Brunswick was up for grabs at the time Cayce gave me the reading.

But Goetz put me in touch with Herman Starr, head of Decca Records, which owned Brunswick Radio and was affiliated with Warners.

Another example of coincidence developed. I outlined my purpose to Starr and told him that I knew this deal would go through because I had Cayce to go by. I also said that I would put Brunswick back on the map as a major trade name in the electronic field.

Starr said he was sorry to have to inform me that I was too late: He was already in the process of selling Brunswick Radio, which had become a costly burden to him. He had found a purchaser, who was to call at a quarter of eleven to close the deal formally.

I did not want to interfere with a deal that was already set. But I wanted Brunswick, and I felt I had a right to buy it if the deal did not go through or if the man did not call.

We reached an accord that the commitment to the other man would be honored if he called by the time he said he would—or within fifteen minutes after the stated time.

Eleven-fifteen came and no phone call. At eleven-thirty I closed the deal and purchased the company. The other buyer called quite some minutes later. Mr. Starr told him that he regretted deeply to inform him that he was too late with his call and the company had been sold to another buyer.

That was how I obtained control of Brunswick Radio and became chairman of the board.

I had all the rights I needed. The Brunswick trademark in the electronic field was mine. We could not make records—or pool tables—under the Brunswick name, but we could make anything electrical.

After obtaining control of this company, I went into partnership with three experts in the electrical field and set up a plant operation in Celina, Ohio. The fields that lay ahead were big —radio, record players, and television.

One step I took was to go to the Metropolitan Museum of Art and study furniture designs. I wanted only the finest for Brunswick and thought we could combine the best traditional cabinet design with the best modern electronic equipment for reproducing sound. And this combination is what we brought to the American scene. We made magnificent reproductions of period furniture—French, Hepplewhite, Sheraton, William and Mary, Chinese, Chippendale, and many others. We made combination radio-phonograph cabinets and cabinets which were the forerunners of the television classic cabinet designs of a later day.

Brunswick was a major operation in which I employed some fifteen hundred workers in several plants in various parts of the United States.

Our lives settled into new patterns, but our work with Cayce and his son Hugh Lynn and the Cayce movement continued with no letup. Many meetings were held in our home with the growing numbers of Cayce followers—and with persons seeking his help. Both Lucille and I were present at Virginia Beach at board meetings and policy discussions.

In 1935 I lost my mother. Her passing left a great gap in our lives. But I never forgot her injunction to me, that I should help this man Cayce and make his work known to the world. Of all of us, Mother had perhaps the most special rapport with Judge. They lived a warm, running friendship over many years of correspondence and meetings. The readings gave her time, she firmly believed, to see the fulfillment of all her dreams for her children.

One of the most extraordinary of Cayce's readings for our family came in connection with the birth of our first son.

Lucille had given up her stage career since Cayce, in his reading for her, had suggested she should choose between her career and her home. In 1929, two years after we were married, she was expecting our first child. I had readings about this situation. There were indications of problems.

In February Lucille was in a room on the maternity floor at Woman's Hospital in New York, waiting for the baby to be born. I was there most of that time with her. We waited for three days. Finally, the doctors came to me and asked if they could perform a Caesarean to relieve the situation and Lucille's pain. I asked for an hour to think about it. They consented. I telephoned Cayce in Virginia Beach and asked for a reading.

The reading, on file at Virginia Beach, begins with a note, typed by Gladys Davis:

"*Background*—See 903–11 on 1–9–29.
2–14–29 Husband phoned from hospital to see if check reading could give any advice to aid birth of baby. He [David E. Kahn] was so concerned that Edgar Cayce gave the reading at 10:20 P.M., which meant that he [EC] would not be able to retire for his normal sleep for some hours yet."

The actual reading was as follows: 903–12 F. 26 yrs. "This psychic reading given by Edgar Cayce at his office, 115 West 35th Street, Virginia Beach, Va., this 14th day of February 1929, in accordance with request made by Mr. David Kahn.

Present: Edgar Cayce; Mrs. Cayce, Conductor; Gladys Davis, Steno; Mrs. Thos. B. House.

Reading:

Time of Reading—Noon . . . Woman's Hospital
10:20 P.M. Eastern Standard Time—110th St., N.Y. City.

MRS. C: You will give the physical condition of this body at the present time, with suggestions for the welfare of the body and that depending on it. You will answer the questions I will ask you regarding same.

MR. C: We have the body [Lucille Kahn] here, and those conditions as surround same. This we have had before. Now, there is near the time of the fulfilment of that as has been given, and while the conditions are outwardly of the extreme nature, to some, the condition is understood by those in charge of same and they should have, as given, their leeway of handling the condition. *The injection of the assistance through the rectum*[1] will be the easier way for mother and child, for while the mother will be in labor for seven to ten hours, this should be accomplished in a nominal, normal manner. Ready for question.

Page 2–903–12

Q.1. Does that mean it will be from seven to ten hours from now before the baby will be born?

A.1. From seven to ten hours from the beginning of labor pains, which began in the afternoon.

Q.2. Will baby be born normally?

A.2. As has been given, it should be—were the correct conditions carried out as ones in charge feel now—though there may arise other conditions from present existent ones. They should not be, with the proper care.

Q.3. Of what should the injection be?

A.3. That as is commonly used for such. The compound of those narcotics used as same.

Q.4. Should anything be said to the doctor in charge?

A.4. As given, the doctor should have charge and not be commanded.

Q.5. What advice to father after baby comes?

A.5. There might be a world of this but just be as patient as can at present.

Q.6. Any further advice concerning this?

A.6. This, and that as is being done, is being done properly at present. We are through for the present."

Although couched in the usual language of Cayce's "forces" this reading as further reported on the telephone definitely

[1] Italics mine—D.K.

indicated that there should be no Caesarean at that time and an injection of narcotics in the rectum would be advisable. The next morning a baby would be born.

I hung up the phone and told the doctor about the Cayce reading. I gave him the full information as to what Cayce had said and explained how Cayce went into the trance state and did not know what he was saying and knew nothing about medicine.

Dr. Samuel Geist, the obstetrician, called in the resident doctor in charge that night and asked, "Doctor, what have you just done?" The resident looked startled and said, "Just as you ordered, Doctor. I gave Mrs. Kahn the rectal injection of narcotics as you specified."

Dr. Geist said, "Let me tell you something. Mr. Kahn just called a man in Virginia Beach named Cayce who told him in a trance reading to give Mrs. Kahn exactly the injection you have just given her."

So impressed was our obstetrician that he stayed in the hospital that night. Cayce was off on the timing, however—the labor was longer than ten hours, actually. But the next morning, without any Caesarean, an eight-and-a-half-pound baby boy was born with no significant difficulties.

We named him S. David Kahn. David was about two weeks old when he had his first reading from the Judge. The reading indicated a number of things that David might successfully interest himself in, one of them being medicine. In the years that followed, David gradually came to know what the readings had indicated. This caused him some difficulty, since it was hard to identify his own interests as separate from the influence of what he had been told. Nonetheless he showed what appeared to be an early interest in both architecture and medicine. Following college, he went on to medical school and then undertook training in psychiatry and psychoanalysis. He married Caroline Phelps who was then working for *The Ladies Home*

Journal. In 1967 they were living in the south and had two children, a boy and a girl. David was teaching and doing research in academic medicine.

Richard, our second son, was born in 1931. The Cayce readings advised that he be given training in law. Richard also attended Harvard College and then went on to Harvard Law School. He married a Radcliffe girl, Judy Raff. They have three sons. Dick is a practicing attorney, a member of a large New York law firm. Both of our sons became members of the board of trustees of the American Society for Psychical Research.

Richard's life reading contains another example of Cayce's remarkable powers. The reading, given when he was five months old, states:

". . . be mindful that there are not those activities of the body in the home, or in play, that will offer the greatest opportunity for injury in the lower limbs, and the period through which this must be mindful of the most, in the third to the fifth year, see, and especially in that period from the middle of October to the middle of August of the next year."

We took whatever precautions we could to guard against the predicted injury. On October 25, 1935, when Dick was four-and-a-half years old, while playing in our home, he pierced the cornea of his right eye with a pair of scissors. Although the reading was off on the part of the body, the accuracy of the date predicted was extraordinary. Between the time of the accident and November of the next year, we had seven readings concerning treatment of the eye. Surgery had been performed immediately to save the eye, but a cataract developed. Although the doctors wanted to operate again to remove the cataract, the readings advised that certain treatments would make further surgery unnecessary. And once again, the readings were right. We followed Cayce's instructions, and the cataract dissolved.

Both boys grew up in a world of shifting excitement with people arriving and leaving at all times of the day and night. They accepted all this as perfectly natural.

It was not at all unusual for the children to be in the room while Mr. Cayce was in trance state giving a reading about someone's previous life—or diagnosing ailments of some patient he had never seen.

Many of the people whom our sons met in those formative years were leaders in the world of science, letters, parapsychology, and metaphysics, and the influence of these men must have helped to shape their careers and their open-mindedness to all things.

CHAPTER 12

Sunset . . . Sunrise . . .

He had guided me safely through one war. Now I would be in a second.

We were older; times had changed. My part in the struggle would be in a different mode, to meet different needs.

Because of its electronic technological experience, my Brunswick company was one of those much-needed firms in defense production for European nations facing the Hitler threat, and for our own armed forces. In all of this Brunswick could play a part. Equally, apart from the company, I would play mine.

Brunswick had put me into the radio manufacturing business with its sound reproduction and transmission techniques. I decided to seek guidance from Cayce on what role we could do best in the emerging war crisis. I wrote him and asked for a reading.

The reading said I should go to Washington, D.C., call Mrs. Roosevelt, and inform her that I would like to meet General Brehon B. Somervell and Secretary of the Treasury Morganthau. I arrived as advised and phoned Miss Thompson, Mrs. Roosevelt's very efficient secretary. She said she would notify

Mrs. Roosevelt as soon as possible and call me back at my hotel.

Ten minutes later Mrs. Roosevelt called and invited me to lunch at the White House at one o'clock. She was always considerate and interested in hearing about her pet project—Arthurdale. She did not mention my requests for meetings, but when I reached my hotel later, there were three messages waiting for me. I met the people I wanted to see and, through them, the officials in charge of purchasing items desperately needed by the government. I was ushered into one office where a colonel in charge had obviously been briefed that I was a trouble shooter who seemed to know how to get whatever was in critically short supply.

The colonel said he had been instructed to put me into the quartz crystal business. I didn't know what quartz crystal was. He explained that it was extremely important in submarine devices and in other vital instrumentation used in defense. He said most of the quartz came from South America. Polished and cut, they sold for about eight dollars apiece. I had an order for eight million. My job was to find the crystals and get them where they were needed within a matter of weeks. He added that it was an almost impossible assignment.

Then certain things began to happen—the unusual incident or coincidence that opened a way, a path ahead, the unlooked-for events that I had come—by association with Judge—to look for.

I consulted with a panel of thirty experts whose job it was to find and expedite the purchase of rare or difficult-to-obtain materials essential to the defense effort. During the meeting, the panel discussed a new rumor that one man in Rio de Janeiro had accumulated large supplies of the quartz but was not shipping any of his stockpiles to America. I asked for his name. To the startled looks of some of the panel members, I picked up the phone, asked for the emergency operator—and called this man in Rio. When he came on the line, I told him, "This is David Kahn in Washington, D.C. Yesterday morning, when I left my home in Scarsdale, I drove your wife and your new baby girl to the station in my car. They're en route to your mother's home in Washington."

The man was amazed and delighted at this unexpected piece of news about his family. He himself had not yet seen the little girl. The mysterious man in Rio was our next-door neighbor in Scarsdale.

We found that the rumor was true. He did have the quartz, five million two-pound boxes of it, outside his windows in Rio, but he had no planes, ships, or other means of transportation to get it out. I said I could arrange that part of it if he could make a binding commitment. He could and did. Two days later two planes left for Rio to begin a daily shuttle between Rio and Miami bringing four thousand pounds of quartz crystal back on every trip.

It is such incidents that make me so sure that my life is not a series of coincidences but an unfoldment.

I sought guidance from Judge and I got it.

Sometimes the guidance was sharp and critical; the alter-ego speaking out of the subconscious would display impatience on some act or word of mine, or would ask me to curb my personal interests if they seemed to overstep the bounds.

Here is part of the dialogue in a reading with Cayce in February 1942, almost two months after Pearl Harbor. Cayce, of course, was in trance:

"*Q.* Would Arthurdale or Rockford, Illinois, be best for me to make ammunitions, such as steel shells?

"*A.* As we find, Arthurdale would be preferable, and there could be easily assembled that necessary for the making of the same, better than the changing over in so much of the activities in Rockford. Because Rockford would be better in anything that has to do with wood working.

"*Q.* Is there anything yet to be done by me to prove my ability to the Treasury?

"*A.* These will stand on what has been accomplished, not what may be said verbally.

"*Q.* How long should I stay in Arthurdale this time?

"*A.* Long enough to tend to the business there. . . ."

The sleeping man speaking out of an unknown plane did not hesitate to say what he had to say. And I—listening—knew how close, how sharp, his words actually were:

"Please give me time and dates for my plan of activity and guidance," I asked at one time, regarding this war development.

"These must come as they are progressed to," he answered. "They MAY not . . . they WILL not be given, until you accomplish it."

More important than anything else during the years of war was my relationship with General Somervell. In the first place, in a life reading, Cayce went deeply into the story of previous incarnations, previous lives on earth. I am aware that many persons question the theories of reincarnation, but I have heard Cayce tell these things and I have come to accept them as the East accepts this concept of birth and rebirth, of progress of the human soul from one lifetime to the next. And the individual entity may—and does—seek out associates of former lives.

In the reading, it was said that in a previous lifetime I had been an aide to Lord Howe, the British general in the American Revolution. Lord Howe, the life reading stated, was a previous incarnation of this same Somervell, with whom I was to work as a civilian aide in the present incarnation.

Cayce had also told me that I would do a great deal of work

for General Somervell, who was in complete charge of all supplies for the United States Army.

But when I met with the general, I did not mention anything about the Cayce reincarnation reading or any previous associations.

I learned from good sources that it had been Harry Hopkins, one of Roosevelt's closest advisers, who had been called by Mrs. Roosevelt and told to make the appointments for me to meet Somervell. The general was a tall, slender man, with a sandy mustache. He said he had a problem. The Army was developing what was to become the USO organization; they wanted rooms in every new camp where recruits could relax and meet with their families and parents when they had the time. This was the start of the program and it was a big job, ultimately involving millions of dollars' worth of furniture. Somervell wanted me to take on the job of purchasing furniture for all these camps. I would have the rank of colonel. He wanted the rooms furnished by Christmas morning—this was already early December 1941.

I told him I didn't want to accept the rank of colonel. I preferred to maintain my civilian status. "There are plenty of colonels outside your office waiting to see you, General," I reminded him. "Being in uniform and having the rank of colonel would present problems." I told him I would be the spokesman for the Army in this matter and make all the contacts and that the job would be done. I told him also, "I promise never to misuse your confidence."

I asked one favor. If anyone criticized me to him, or accused me of any kind of misbehavior, I wanted a chance to answer. I had to be as realistic as I could; I was a civilian, I was Jewish, and in working directly with a general, I would be going over the heads of a lot of people. I told him, "If you make a mistake, they say that SOB Somervell. If I make one, they say that Jew bastard Kahn."

The general said, "You see that door? That is my private door. You come in that door until I tell you not to come."

Furniture had been my business too long for me not to know the ropes, even when it meant trying to buy hundreds of sofas and chairs and other reception room furnishings in a matter of a few days. I did it through the New York Furniture Exchange, picking the best-looking pieces I could buy in large quantities, and had the complete rooms set up for the general's inspection at the Furniture Exchange. Everyone saw and everyone was delighted. And a few weeks later the general told me, "Congratulations on that beautiful job." Then he added, "I have another job for you."

It was about a new steel item. The Army needed immediately five million steel links used to hold belts of bullets so that a machine gun could fire seven hundred times a minute.

I went across the street and met a general who turned me over to the colonel in charge of the Watertown, Massachusetts, arsenal. I sat down with some of the brass connected with the Watertown operation and we talked it over. For five hours these men tried their damnedest to unsell me on the whole idea. I said to the colonel, "What would you do if a general gave you an order?"

He grinned and said, "I'd break my so-and-so trying to do it."

I told him that was what we were up against. This was what the general wanted.

By the end of that day I had the plan underway. I was to visit six large manufacturers in various parts of the country and arrange for buying new equipment, furnaces, and steel. I took a member of the War Production Board and three engineers from the S. W. Farber company in Long Island City. The Farber company manufactured very fine kitchenware. Perhaps it did not sound like the most likely firm to make machine-gun links by the millions but I knew its work and the performance of the people. The head of the firm, who had come to this country from Austria, was an expert in metals; he told me we should use a high-carbon steel like that used in watches for the machine-gun links. We had difficulties to overcome all the way, to get the tools we needed made, and made right, and to get space, which was at a premium. We took over a geranium hothouse on Long Island for two thousand dollars a month and covered the entire dirt floor with concrete. Within three months we were turning out a million links a day. Our reject links were down to one-tenth of one per cent. We had designed a whole new link that proved so successful it became the standard in the production of this extremely important product and won the Army-Navy "E" award.

My relationship with the general was one of warmth, trust, and friendship. Whenever I needed any help or support I had only to call him or his secretary—by coincidence again, I had known her when I first came to Washington in World War I. Her help was often invaluable for America. Once four nimble-fingered Italian-Americans who were expert at making machine-gun links were about to be drafted. I appealed to the colonel in charge of induction to let them stay and turn out those links. The colonel was adamant. "By tomorrow," he said, "your friends will be in the service. . . ."

I tried to explain that I didn't even know them but I needed them, the country needed them. When he refused to listen, I picked up the phone and called Miss Katie in the general's office. I told her to put the men's names on lists of those to be sent in uniform the next day to the Farber plant. The colonel was furious when he learned of this and told me so. But I said, "You did your duty. So now I do mine. These men will save more lives and produce more in the Farber factory than they would overseas."

The fifty-caliber machine gun was one of the most effective

weapons our armed forces had. It helped to shorten the war, perhaps more than any other weapon. The link we made was one of the most important contributions to this weapon.

The shooting war was on the front lines in Europe and the Pacific. The production war was on the front lines at home. Our links were always marked with a "B" with a circle around it. I remember that during a wartime convention of manufacturers a lieutenant colonel just back from the fighting wanted to know who made the links with that mark. I thought he had some complaint and said "I make them. What's the problem?"

He said there was no problem. He said our link with the "B" was the kind the men at the front preferred and that we should be turning out more and more. The manufacturers went to see the process in operation at what we still called the "Geranium Hothouse." Their understanding of our techniques helped tremendously in production.

We needed electric furnaces to "cook" the link. I called up friends at General Electric; they said it would take about seven months. Westinghouse said it would take six months.

Every morning I commuted to the plant from Scarsdale on the train and often rode with Charley Wilson, who was really the boss of General Electric. I told him the problem and Charley called Erie, Pennsylvania, and later called me and said, "Dave, on Sunday morning you'll have a staff of engineers in your plant and you'll have those furnaces within six weeks." And we did.

In our plants—we ultimately had one in Long Island City and one in Brooklyn—we turned out a million and a half of those links a day, every day, for the duration of the war.

Throughout those war years and the pursuits that kept me so busy much of the time, I found myself increasingly concerned about Judge and his own strenuous activities. He still led two lives: The prophet asleep—in trance—speaking out of his shadowed room of what he called the Akashic records; and, on the other side, the plain man of the farm, the man bent over his flowers, working over his fruit preserves, which were truly wonderful. A gentle man, who accepted himself for what he was at both levels of reality.

But the war years were years of struggle, of life and death, and Cayce caught the intensity of the period, and instead of taking on fewer cases and readings, he took on more. Many of these readings he would give in Scarsdale when he, Gertrude, and Gladys would stay in our home.

The strain became tremendous until it was finally agreed that he would go away to recover his strength. In the reading he gave about himself he responded to the question as to how long he would be gone from Virginia Beach with the answer, "Until he is well or dead."

I knew that he had been overdoing phsyically and I think emotionally under the strain of those months. When I was with him at Virginia Beach he would complain more and more about his "gizzard acting up." He went away to a kind of residence associated with a medical clinic. One day I got a call from Judge's wife Gertrude in Roanoke, Virginia.

Gertrude told me on the phone that Judge had had a slight stroke. "He wants to go home," she told me.

I told her to tell Judge I would be there in the morning. When I arrived at the hotel, Cayce was in a wheel chair. He had a paralytic condition on his right side, the result of the stroke.

I never saw Judge like this. He wept. He told me what he had been going through, his suffering. Gertrude was very badly shaken by it. I told them not to worry; it would all work out, it would all be resolved.

I talked with Judge's friend, Dr. Henry George, III, in Wilmington, Delaware, and arranged, at the physician's suggestion, to have an ambulance take Judge to a hospital in

Wilmington. But Judge wanted to go home. He was a man of strong will. The ambulance took him not to Wilmington but back to Virginia Beach.

I did not ride with Judge in the ambulance. And, tragically, I was not to see my friend again. He returned to the beach, to the sands in whose therapeutic power he so deeply believed, to the ocean, the waves, the salt winds, to all of which he had been guided by his forces.

A month later, on January 3, 1945, Judge died. Burial was in his family plot in Hopkinsville, Kentucky.

Three months later, Gertrude, his wife, who had shared so many years of Cayce's life, joined her husband in that other realm. Death came Easter Sunday morning, precisely at sunrise.

CHAPTER 13

There Is a River.

Like so much that happened in Cayce's life, the development of the book called *There Is a River* by Thomas Sugrue, which was to carry the Cayce story to thousands of persons across the world, came in a wholly unexpected, unlooked-for way. Yet it emerged and shaped out of much that was a part of Cayce's life, including the role of his son, Hugh Lynn, of myself, and, perhaps above all, of Lucille.

But I must begin with a word about Tom Sugrue himself. Truly one of the most gifted journalists of our times, he wrote his works under the most difficult physical conditions any writer ever had to overcome. And Tom would never have dreamed, while he was Hugh Lynn Cayce's roommate in college, that he would have written anything favorable about his roommate's psychic father.

Sugrue was born in Naugatuck, Connecticut. He was Irish and gifted with a fine literary and journalistic talent. At Washington and Lee University, he roomed with Hugh Lynn. They were—particularly at that time—very different types. Sugrue was imbued with a Roman Catholic background and upbringing. And he was also a sound journalist even then. He wanted facts, not wild claims, about so-called forces from which Edgar Cayce drew cosmic secrets.

Conflict between the two young men began almost as soon as they started discussing their religious ideas. It was much more than merely the fact that Sugrue was Catholic and young Cayce, Southern Presbyterian. (The Cayces had joined the Presbyterian Church in Virginia Beach.) It was also Hugh Lynn's father, who, to Sugrue's mind, had to be at the best a case of self-deception, despite all the protestations of Hugh Lynn to the contrary.

For days they would not even speak to each other. They liked each other—but each felt the significance of his own ideas. Each wanted the other to understand. As young men with strong feelings they could not compromise. At last one day Hugh Lynn suggested, "Tom, why don't you come home with me this weekend, meet my family, and hear Dad give one of those readings?"

Sugrue said, "Sure, Hugh Lynn, I'll go down there with you. And I'll show you it isn't—it can't be—what you say."

So the pair set out for Virginia Beach, Sugrue certain he would uncover a real fraud that anyone with an objective approach could spot. But Hugh Lynn arranged a reading for Tom and when it was finished, in the face of details about himself that no one could have told Cayce, Tom looked from this gangly man to his son and declared, "This is the most remarkable thing I have ever seen or heard."

It was the beginning of a new relationship and new religious liberalism in Tom. He became a part of the Cayce family; he lived with them in the summer, spent weekends with them, and helped out in every way he could. When they were graduated, Hugh Lynn, who did not expect things to be handed to him, but who did want to continue the work of his father in whatever way he could, started out with a job in the Atlantic

University library, at Virginia Beach. Tom decided to go to New York. He had majored in journalism and was hoping to break into that field. He was interviewed by the *Herald-Tribune* and given a summer fill-in job as a reporter. Eventually he went on the staff full time and began to attract attention with his by-line stories.

One of Tom's stories was an interview with Cardinal Spellman. This was so incisive and revealing a portrait of the Catholic prelate that the editor of the *American* magazine, Sumner Blossom, engaged Tom as a full-time roving reporter who could go anywhere in the world so long as he turned in one story a month. It was a big break for Tom, and when I heard of it I told him to be sure of only one thing: "If they ever fire you—make certain you have a letter that guarantees you return passage home from wherever you happen to be."

Whether it was destiny—or karma—or whatever it might be called, this assignment was the undoing and in another way the shaping of his whole life. Tom went to Italy first, journeyed to the top of a high mountain to visit a monastery centuries old, and wrote a fine story about these monks on the mountaintop. Then he traveled east to Arabia. Eager to get an authentic story he asked his Egyptian guide to take him into his own home and let him meet and dine with his family. This the guide agreed to do. At the evening meal, as was customary, everyone drank from the same cup and dipped into the main dish with their fingers. From this time on Tom gradually began to develop a physical disability that began in the knee joints—a difficulty in moving.

As time went on, the condition worsened. Lucille, who had come to look on Tom as a writer of extraordinary gifts, became deeply concerned with helping him. Cayce, of course, gave readings. Tom, however, had married a lovely Catholic girl and at first she discouraged him about the readings because her religion did not approve of this kind of psychic activity.

After many months, Tom tried a new kind of fever therapy, involving a coffin-like box lined with electric bulbs, designed to raise the temperature artificially and burn out the germs. Tom was stretched out in this contraption with everything but his head covered in the terrific heat. It was a new technique, they said. For Tom, it was disaster.

It left him greatly weakened. After that, his wife Mary realized that there was no alternative to the Cayce readings. Tom lived in the Cayce home with Hugh Lynn nursing him from 1939 to 1941. He then went with his wife and little daughter to Clearwater, Florida, where the treatment continued. Cayce gave him many treatments, including sodium of gold, cobra venom, and other things that were ahead of their time.

During this two-year period, Tom devoted himself to one cause—writing the story of Cayce. Most of this book was written under the most difficult physical conditions and limited mobility. It was written and rewritten, but the finished product has become one of the classics in the field of modern metaphysics.

In his life of Cayce, Tom understood, as few other human beings did or could, the meanings of Cayce and of the often enigmatic words of the thousands of readings.

His interpretations of some of the readings, in *There Is a River,* revealed the depth of Tom's own awareness, his grasp of birth and rebirth, of the karmic principle of retribution, and the importance of the cosmic speck called a human being.

"The plan for the soul included experience of all creations," he wrote in his book, "but it did not necessarily mean identification with and participation in all forms and substance. Nor did it mean interference in creation by souls. It did not mean that they were to spin their own little worlds, twisting and bending laws to make images of their dreams.

"But these things could happen. The soul was the greatest

thing that was made; it had free will. Once free will was given, God did nothing to curb it; however it acted, it had to act within Him; by whatever route, it had to return to Him. . . ."

Judge gave Tom a number of readings about the book—one of them stated that Henry Holt and Company should be the publishers. Cayce did not know one publisher from the other. But the book was taken to Holt and was published by Holt. They wanted a book, they said, that would tell the world about Cayce for the first time.

Sugrue's story gave the world its first life-size look at this remarkable individual. It was to sell hundreds of thousands of copies in hard cover and soft. It has kindled an interest in the man I knew as Judge that has spread across the world.

Tom wrote a number of other books. Despite his difficulties, he was a vibrant human being who felt life and everything it had to offer was worthwhile. He believed in reincarnation. He believed that he was working out his karma in this life for what he had done or failed to do in other lifetimes. He examined all the ideas of religion carefully, frankly, honestly. He wrote a book called *A Catholic Speaks His Mind on America's Religious Dilemma* in which he questioned many of the materialistic aspects of the church's organization and theology. Much of what he then criticized has since been changed by later ecumenical actions of church authorities.

When he was not in Virginia Beach, he often stayed with us. He had his own room in our house. Both Lucille and I loved him and cared for him. We would often go out with him to dinner or the theater. He could write and speak, his mind was clear and sharp, and his heart and soul full of the beauty of words and meanings. But much of the time he was all but physically helpless.

Lucille with her care gave him at least fifteen years of added joy in New York. When we went to a theater, we had to have help in getting him in and out of a taxi or car because he could not bend his knees, waist, or neck. Then the cab driver and I would get him back into the house after the show. With these problems, he and Lucille were still able to develop a radio program called "Conversation at Eight" which was put on weekly for several months over station WINS.

There Is a River was written from 1939 to 1942. This was followed by his second book, *Starling of the White House,* a book that involved both Judge and myself—and some of the most startling coincidences in publishing history.

Bill Starling was born in Hopkinsville and had been a friend of Edgar Cayce throughout his life. He had become the top secret service man in the White House and the protector of presidents from Theodore Roosevelt to Franklin Roosevelt. When Cayce and I were in Washington on one occasion, he took me to meet Starling. During the Arthurdale period, I worked closely with the White House. Starling and I were friends.

In the early months of World War II Starling told me he was tired and was anxious to retire. Louis Howe, one of President Roosevelt's closest advisers, had just died from overwork. Starling said he didn't want to be carried out feet first like Louis. He had a talk with the President who agreed to let Starling retire as of October 1, 1942. Then, Starling said, he wanted to write his book. It would tell the story of his years in the White House. Starling said at that time, "Dave, I want you to handle this book."

I pointed out that I wasn't a writer and suggested that he take one of the Washington newsmen he had come to know so well over these years. He said no, he wanted me to handle this project and he knew that we had the blessing of Mr. and Mrs. Roosevelt.

"Bill," I said, "much as I'd like to do this, for your sake I wouldn't undertake it unless you'll go with me to Virginia Beach and let Cayce give a reading."

Starling had known Cayce all these years and had never had a reading. Now he consented to my plan, and we traveled to Virgina Beach. Judge was startled to see the pair of us and said to Starling, "Bill, what are you doing here?"

I explained that we had come down to get a reading. Cayce was at the moment involved in opening mail. Margueritte Bro, a prominent writer and editor in the religious field, had written an article for a popular magazine on Cayce and tens of thousands of letters had poured into Cayce's office.

I told Judge we had to get information for Bill about the future. Judge lay down on his back and gave us the reading. The date was August 29, 1943. He told us that the book should be a strong and impartial story. We had told him nothing about any book before Judge went into trance. It would be ready in the spring and at least 100,000 people would buy it. The reading said that Kahn should finance the book and Simon and Schuster should publish it.

The reading was incredibly specific. It described what the book should be, the high tone and standard it should take. He warned that it had to be above politics, that it should emphasize only the finest meanings. "Do not present any political factions. For, as the entity in its capacities acted—and is acting—in the capacity for the love of God and country—and the man directing the affairs of the nation perchance using the opportunity—as observed by a servant of the people—to the glory of God. That is the manner of presentation of this entity's service to the nation."

In response to questions, the reading gave a virtual outline of the book's whole thrust and direction:

Q. What is best "main appeal" to the editor and reader?
A. The service of a servant to a nation. This has not been

—this is not—trying to make a flowery speech. . . . Why SHOULDN'T it be presented then, as the experience of a servant of the people for the GLORY of God and to the service of his fellow man?

Q. Would that be a good central theme for the book?

A. Isn't that what has just been given?

Q. Who would be the best publisher to do the job?

A. As we find, a serial in such as *Collier's;* published [as book] by such as Simon and Schuster.

Q. What is best approach to Simon and Schuster?

A. Just that it may be written. They're looking and waiting for it.

It was interesting that the reading said Simon and Schuster, where earlier he had given us Holt as the publisher of *There Is a River*. Why the change? And why the statement that "they're looking and waiting for it?"

We had no answer at that time.

The reading went on to say that Tom Sugrue would be a good choice as the writer, but it said that Sugrue would best remain in Clearwater until "at least the outline is set." The situation afterward would depend, said the reading, "on general circumstances." It is true that Tom had had some earlier associations with Simon and Schuster. But he had these same associations when Cayce's reading had sent him to Henry Holt with *There Is a River*.

The Starling book, the reading said, would aid the post-war situation still to come.

Regarding how much should be said about visitors to the White House in that wartime era, especially those known to Bill Starling, it went on: "Enough to indicate the needs of warnings. This is to the fellow man! Not to laud any particular president, but principles—principles! Not to belittle any, as it will not be the purpose of the individual entity here presenting same; nor should it be sarcastic nor anything bordering on the same, by the one writing the story. The truth, sure—but PRINCIPLE first! And it will be, then, not merely a best seller but—for many years—the ideal of many an American."

All of this detailed discussion and outline of a book was given by a man who had not known what we were going to ask about when he went into trance.

And also, of some interest to us, he predicted a best seller—even more than "merely a best seller."

Following the reading, Starling returned to Washington, and I continued on to New York, arriving about one o'clock on a Saturday morning in the middle of a rainstorm. I went to the cab stand and finally got a taxi.

A large number of people were waiting for cabs, and I realized it wasn't fair for me to take the cab alone at such an hour and in such weather. I saw a tall man carrying a black suitcase on his shoulder. I called out, "You with the black bag on your shoulder. You going uptown?"

The man stopped, turned, and said, "Yes, I am."

"Come along, I'll give you a lift," I called back.

I hadn't noticed this man on the train. He put his bag in the cab and said, "My name's Schuster."

Since I had heard Cayce name Simon and Schuster only hours before, I said, "You wouldn't, by any chance, be the Schuster of Simon and Schuster?"

And he said, "Yes, I'm Max Schuster."

I told him my name and that I lived in New York. Then I stated that I was glad I had run into him because he was going to publish a book for me.

Mr. Schuster seemed a little startled. Without any great show of enthusiasm, he asked me what this book he was going to publish was about. I told him the title was *Starling of the White House.*

Now he looked really surprised. "You mean Bill Starling?"

I said, "Yes, I do."

He then told me that Bill Starling had put him into the Senate as a page boy when Schuster was a kid twelve or fourteen years old. He said, "But why didn't Bill come direct to us?"

So then I told him my story, about Edgar Cayce and the reading he had given Bill, and about Tom Sugrue, whom Schuster said was a wonderful writer who had once ghost written a story for his publishing firm.

Tom did the book. It was published a year after *There Is a River* and was, again as Cayce predicted, a best seller for many months.

Simon and Schuster published a widely discussed advertisement with the banner head "How a Best Seller Is Born." In an advertisement unique in publishing, it documented and described the events leading up to the publication—including the reading at Virginia Beach directing Bill and me to go to Simon and Schuster, and my encounter with Schuster at the railroad station in New York in the small hours of the following morning.

Bill Starling lived long enough to know that the book was finished and on the presses. But the strains of the job he told about in the book had been too heavy. He died three weeks before publication.

Tom Sugrue did other books in the years that followed. I think, again because she was so close to him and his story, that Lucille should tell her part of it in her own words:

"I met Tom in 1927 while he was at Washington and Lee University. He was visiting Hugh Lynn at the time of my first trip to Virginia Beach with Dave shortly after we were married. Tom and I immediately clicked. It was as if we had always known each other. It remained that way all his life; we had a unique relationship. And we asked Mr. Cayce to give us a reading on where we had been together before. He said that Tom and I had been in India together in a previous incarnation. We both had had our greatest spiritual unfoldment in that life. This we accepted as our bond.

"From Clearwater Beach, he wrote letters filled with a poignant longing to return to New York. His zest for living, for contacts with all his colleagues, had not diminished because of his disability. Dave and I sought out one of our oldest friends, Jack Cominsky of the *Saturday Review of Literature*. He had also known Tom during his newspaper days. Jack had been losing many of his best men to the war and we helped him to realize that even though Tom was in a wheel chair, this did not in the least affect his ability as a writer. Despite misgivings about the problems Tom might encounter in finding a place to live accessible to the offices of the magazine, Jack agreed to bring him back to the city and put him on the staff.

"This was still wartime and it was difficult to find a place for Tom to live. Dave and I went to the Seymour Hotel, across the street from the offices on Forty-fourth Street. They accepted Tom and his family with no problems whatever. Dave remarked to us, when the Lord wants something to happen the impossible becomes possible."

As Lucille states, he was always close to us. His association with Lucille and me deepened his interest in the Jewish people and their faith and their struggle to establish their homeland in Israel. Through Ben Abrams of Emerson Radio and others it was made possible for Tom to go to Israel and do a book on the heroic struggle of the Jews in our own time. Harpers agreed to publish. A young editor who agreed to accompany Tom on the trip fell ill aboard ship and had to come home.

Terribly crippled, curbing his pain with continual doses of aspirin, Tom was still not about to give up his assignment. In

Italy, Tom caught a refugee plane out of Germany and proceeded to Israel alone. We arranged for people to be with him all the time he was there. He was taken from Dan to Beersheba, a seriously disabled man, a Roman Catholic come to Israel to see its people and its story at first hand. He wrote ecstatically of his adventures.

He spent about nine months in the Holy Land. He was there for the first birthday of the new Israel. Ben and his wife, Betty, and Lucille and I went to Israel for that celebration. Tom had become part of the whole country and especially its people—from all the oppressed countries of Europe.

Wherever he went he was cared for. He did not complain even when things were difficult. He could not move himself and one night in a hotel the roof leaked and water dripped on him all night long. When his nurse arrived in the morning, she found him lying helpless on a drenched mattress.

It was difficult and hard for him and yet in a way it was one of his greatest hours as a reporter, an author. Wherever he went people knew him; he was among them and of them. He was a special kind of hero in a land of many heroes.

Again, let Lucille tell this part in her own words:

"Tom had finished his book on Israel, *Watch for the Morning*. He was giving a talk in New York before a group of medical doctors in a Bonds for Israel drive and met a famous orthopedic surgeon, who agreed to give his services to Tom at no cost if funds could be raised for a long rehabilitation program in hospitals. A number of Tom's friends got together and raised a large sum and Tom went to the hospital. They were going to operate first on one hip. Tom could not bend from the waist because of a fused bone condition. By that time except for his shoulders, fingers and his eyes, the rest of his body was completely frozen.

"He had been taking cortisone, which was new then. Tom chose to be a guinea pig with the drug. It did relieve the pain and he had a very productive period writing and doing reviews.

"They finally operated and inserted what amounted to an artificial joint to give mobility to the hip. But when he tried to move his leg he cried out in agony because he had not moved those muscles in years. He was ill for nine weeks, with one crisis after another, and lapsed into deep coma.

"He was in coma for some time. Near the end I was alone in the room with him. During the weeks of illness before the coma I often massaged his legs and toes; he said this gave him relief from the pain. Now, standing at the foot of the bed, I was massaging the leg even though he was in coma.

"Suddenly I looked up and saw his eyes were open wide and looking at me. I knew he was saying with his eyes, 'Thank you. I know you are here.'

"It was only a moment, but I had that moment and its memory.

"It was the last time I saw him in this lifetime."

CHAPTER 14

Of Dreams and Visions

Dreams have always held a place in our psychic life. Many times since Judge's death I have dreamed of him—and each dream takes on a cloak of reality for me; Judge told me many times in life that whatever happened to him, he would be with me, and would guide me.

Judge did not think of dreams merely as physical, chemical, and psychological. The dream was far more than that to him. It was a channel of communication—of information and meaning—between entities, minds, planes of experience, the conscious and the unconscious interweaving in symbolic metaphysical drama.

Particularly after Judge's death, however, I found dreams of significance coming to me, dreams that involved Cayce himself. This has happened to me over a number of years. Often in the past I discussed my dreams with him when I felt they were significant. These he would interpret in various ways.

In one reading I had asked Judge about a complex and confusing dream of violence and accusations; his answer broke in before I had finished the question: "This as we find is a cross section of more than one experience or vision, and there will come knowledge as concerning some conditions that have been indicated in the vision—which would indicate the needs of circumspect activity on the part of self as well as on the part of those who it will be necessary for the body to counsel and advise. . . ."

It was dreams that brought Cayce to me following his passing. I believed in the afterlife, but I avoided so-called "spirit seances." I was sure that many of these, if not most, were simply frauds. Although I was quite willing to accept the possibility of communication through a true medium, I found that seances were often only an indication of the alleged medium's ability to use knowledge acquired about the subject to make accurate deductions from the subject's behavior and words, or to use any telepathic gifts the subject might have.

Cayce declared in a reading that the experience of dreams may be a "foreshadowing of conditions" that are to come and comparison of the conditions with those this soul "has passed in its evolution to the present sphere."

In another reading, published in an ARE document, Judge was asked by the subject of the reading if the subject's dreams revealed any significant spiritual awakening. Cayce replied:

"As has been experienced by the entity, there are dreams and there are visions and there are experiences. When only dreams, they are also significant but they pertain rather to the physical health or physical condition. In visions, the inter-between—the subconscious mind—gives expression to that which makes for the awakening between the mental consciousness and what has been turned over and over in the physical consciousness. This is a weighing with what you hold as an ideal.

"In visions where there are spiritual awakenings, most often there are symbols or signs. In training yourself to interpret your visions, you must understand in your own language the meanings of all the expressions of eye, hand, mouth, posture, or the like. When the visions, then, are in such symbols, know that the awakening is at hand." (262–9)[1]

Cayce told me many times that whatever happened, communications between us would continue. He did not say this would always come in dreams, but this was the way the communication seems to come.

I have had many such dreams, sometimes cryptic, sometimes quite clear in their implications. Usually, they come at 3 A.M. Perhaps this is the time at which I am most rested and receptive. I knew, of course, that one can dream something merely because of excess eating or because the subconscious is feeding back ideas of sublimated fears or desires, but these dreams were always different. I have had them often, and I get up and write them down.

One instance occurred at a time when I was involved in a difficult business situation in North Carolina. I had taken an option to buy a factory which I planned to use for the construction of Brunswick radio cabinets. A friend of mine named Ed Nicholas, who made radio sets and phonographs for the Capehart people, offered to buy a one-half interest in this plant from me for the price I had optioned to pay for the whole plant.

I agreed. I told him we'd be building cabinets together in ninety days. I kept the former owner of the plant as vice-president in charge of operations. Shortly after this deal with Nicholas was completed, I had a phone call from Ed. It was curt and abrupt: "This is Ed Nicholas. I want to see you tomorrow morning at the St. Regis Hotel."

I asked what it was about and he said, "I don't want to talk about it on the phone."

[1] Figures are filing code identifying the name of the individual for whom the reading is given and the number of the specific reading for this individual. (D.K.)

I told Lucille about it after I hung up. I could not understand why after all these years he would call and ask for a command performance. Neither of us could make any sense out of that call.

That night, when I went to bed, I made a suggestion to myself that I would get an answer. At three in the morning I had this experience: I dreamed that I was on a bridge going out into the Atlantic Ocean. It was pitch dark. I walked out to the end of the bridge and it was open into the sea. I cannot swim. I was frightened. I looked over to the beach and there was Cayce, laughing. Sunshine was all around him and I was still in the dark. Out rolled a huge staircase to where I was standing and I walked down into the sunlight. I asked him what in the world happened. He said, "Don't worry, everything is all right." He said he had told me that death would not part us. When I needed help he would be there. This was one of those times.

I told Cayce that if I did not wake up and write this down I would forget it. So I made a deal with him: "When I wake up in the morning and put the razor to my face to shave, you will remind me of this entire conversation and I will call my secretary, Mrs. Elizabeth Brown, in North Carolina, and dictate this entire dream to her."

When I arose the next morning and put the razor to my face the whole thing illuminated itself in my mind and I went to the telephone and began to make the call. Lucille told me, as I was dialing, that she knew I was going to call Mrs. Brown and what I was going to tell her.

She said, "You had a dream at 3 A.M. this morning in which Edgar Cayce talked with you. . . ."

The dream had been so real—I had actually said all these things to Cayce—out loud. Lucille had heard this whole dream-speak in the pre-dawn darkness.

When I called my secretary, she was disturbed because it

appeared that the former owner had heard about my arrangement with Ed Nicholas and was angry about it, and had told Ed Nicholas just how he felt.

Nicholas, however, was not angry at me. He wanted to tell me about his meeting with the other man and to reassure me that our deal from first to last had been totally proper and that, while he could understand the other man's annoyance, there was not a single reason to take exception to a perfectly proper business transaction.

Listening to this I realized the force of that dream, the darkness, sunlight, and the peril and the laughing face of Judge on the sunlit beach.

I was, indeed, walking down the stairs into the sunlight—precisely because Nicholas understood my true role.

Prophecy, too, came in dreams, a fact that has been evidenced over many centuries, yet it is still a much debated issue, particularly in medical and psychological circles.

In an earlier chapter, I noted that Cayce had predicted the stock market crash in one of my readings but I had not heeded his warning.

Cayce made this prediction several times in the months before the break came in 1929, a number of these predictions having been based on his own interpretations of prophetic dreams brought to him by others for an explanation of the meaning.

Many years after the market crash, Hugh Lynn Cayce, conducting a class on dreams at ARE headquarters in Virginia Beach, described those dreams and readings about the stock crash and the dates on which they took place:

"Early in 1925 Edgar Cayce began stressing in his readings the importance of dreams. Various members of the association, which then sponsored his work, secured readings which gave interpretations of their dreams.

"On March 5 and April 6, 1929, one of these members . . . sent in the following by telephone:

"'Dreamed we should sell all our stocks including box stock (one considered very good). I saw a bull following my wife who was dressed in red.'

"About this Edgar Cayce's reading suggests the following:

"'This is an impression of a condition which is to come about, a downward movement of long duration, not allowing latitude for those [stocks] which are considered very safe. Dispose of all held, even box, signifies great change to come.'

"On April 6, 1929 [the same member] submitted the following dream:

"'A young man was blaming me for murder of a man. A gangster asked, "Is there anyone else in the world who knows this?" I answered, "Mr. Cornell." Saw dead man. The gangster started to administer poisonous hypodermic which had been used on dead man. I felt needle and expected death.

"'Awoke and then went back to sleep. Dreamed interpretation: This represented fight going on in Reserve Board–stock stimulation.'

"Edgar Cayce reading given same day, April 6, 1929, included:

"'There must surely come a break where there will be panic in the money centers, not only of Wall Street's activity but a closing of the boards in many other centers and readjustment of the actual specie–higher and lower quotations to continue for several moons while adjustments are being made–then break.' (On October 29, 1929, sixteen million shares changed hands. By end of 1929 stock losses were estimated at fifteen billion dollars, affecting twenty-five million persons.)"

Dreams and visions were the building blocks of Cayce's

"other life" and its form and definition. It was a world beyond a world; shaped of beauty and poetry, of symbology and meaning.

It was in this connection that Cayce brought in the story of what he called the Akashic records. This is the picture brought to him in his own dreams—slightly changed each time—of a roomless room—where a figure stands—holding a giant volume in which are the records of time and of the souls of the world; all deeds, all thoughts, all words, all dreams, all hopes, fears, justices, even thought or dreamed or felt, are recorded here.

He drew, as he said in the readings, on sources not available to us all. When I asked how we would know all of this, he would say, "Out of the Akashic records."

What are these records, and how and where are they to be found?

According to Cayce, the Akashic records are the records on an entity's existence from the birth of the soul. The records contain the history of the entity's many experiences on earth in different forms and at different times. The idea of these permanent records of all human life is an ancient one; the term *Akashic* is derived from Sanskrit. The records exist beyond conscious experience, beyond the limits of time and space, in the eternal and universal level of existence of the soul and the spirit of God. Cayce's "forces" from this level of existence gave him the ability to read from those records those parts which affected the present life of the soul he was concerned with.

In my long relationship with Cayce and in the hundreds of readings I heard and saw and conducted with Judge, I heard him discuss this phase of his psychic reality and use it directly as he gave the reading. I can recall, especially in the life readings, the way he would speak of these records in trance. Judge would begin, "Now we have the body." And this was 1917. And he would say, "1917—16—15—14 . . ." And he'd go back to 1900 and say, "He was born in 1900, and I'd like to see his records."

In the scene he described, the figure holding the records would lift its hand to turn these pages. And Cayce's reading would go on: "Well, this was in 1775 . . ." as he told me in my own life reading, when he said I was an aide to Lord Howe in England, and he went into some detail in such decriptions. And his one answer when asked about where he obtained all this was, "Out of the records."

The Akashic records remain today among the more obscure areas of the Cayce story. He could not, or in any case did not, reveal much about them except that they were there, that they could be called on. One of the tasks still in progress at the Association for Research and Enlightenment in Virginia Beach is to collate all references to the Akashic records and search for further information about them.

Dreams and visions have been a part of life and of religion from the beginning of time itself. They are found in all the records of life, from the earliest records of men, from the earliest legends, written or unwritten. Dreams and visions are a part of our lives; they were a part of Cayce and his life work. They were a part of mine. Even years after Judge was gone.

CHAPTER 15

Yesterday . . . and Tomorrow

"And in the one before this," Cayce would say, "we find in the Egyptian forces, when the force of law was being given to the people. . . ."

So begins a fragment of a life reading as Cayce, quiet, reposed, reached back into time to relate the records of previous lives of an individual.

The life readings, probing the past history of the entity, past experiences across time, a learning time, perhaps, on this earth, began in late 1923.

It was a strange journey, motionless on the couch, shoeless, asleep, speaking out of the void across centuries and ages, back to forgotten eras, to long-destroyed civilizations of the earth, to lost levels of Atlantis, to sunken temples and crumbling cathedrals drowned in bottomless seas.

In the readings, delving into the past incarnations of individuals, Cayce found continuing relationships of individuals, not coincidental, but part of a pattern, soul seeking soul. A reading about himself revealed that Judge and I had been together in a previous sojourn in Egypt.

This Cayce reading on his own present and past lives declared that he had been in the Egyptian incarnation "one chosen as the highest authority in the mental attitudes, acting in the way of the Priest of the people, being the first chosen priest of the cult, as afterwards called among the nations of the world. . . ." However, the reading states that the entity fell into disgrace because of falling away from virtue and "through this fleshly carnal force brought destructive elements to the entity. . . ."

In my own life reading, of which the following are excerpts with explanations, this story was reflected in the description of the role that the reading said I played. Here the term "entity" refers not to Cayce, but to myself as the subject of the reading:

"Arsha [Kahn] . . . when divisions arose on account of conditions arising in temple. Entity [Kahn] then of priesthood, and offering strange fire upon the altar. Was in defense of the priest driven into exile by aggrandizement of self-interest and fleshing desires; entity though remaining faithful . . .

"The entity then was very close to Edgar Cayce during this period, Cayce being the priest driven into exile. At the present time there is that strong attachment, which has persisted, as before. . . ."

My own life reading not only stated that I had worked for Lord Howe in England, and that this was a previous incarnation of the man I came to know at this time as General Somervell, but that I was an Irishman by the name of O'Harrihan—"aide to the general, in the name of Howe, when America was in rebellion against the yoke. . . ."

From a position of perhaps ignorance about reincarnation, I have come to understand it as a clear path, a road of reality which many souls follow across many lifetimes and worlds. I have even come to believe that Jesus Christ has been reincarnated many times. I have no way of proving this, but I believe it.

Over many years, after Cayce began the life readings, I had

one given—with their full knowledge—for every executive I engaged in many of my business activities. The patterns of their lives worked out almost always in accordance with these readings of previous lives, trainings, needs, fulfillment. When I was first forging ahead in business, a young lady came to me for work, an intelligent girl of about eighteen with a very good high school record. Cayce said she had been with me before. He said she had been extremely loyal to me in past experiences. So I employed this young lady. She remained in my employ and as a friend for forty years.

The Occidental world finds difficulty in accepting the idea of reincarnation. Yet in so many instances with Cayce's life readings, the people involved and the facts in this present lifetime bore out past history connections given in the life reading. There are approximately twenty-five hundred of these readings and the "coincidences" relating to them are too extraordinary to be lightly discounted or dismissed.

An example is the case of Ludwig Stern, manufacturer of pipes in New York City. Mrs. Stern was a very beautiful woman much interested in the work of Cayce and the stories she had heard me tell about him. She and a friend telephoned Cayce in Virginia Beach and made an appointment with him for a reading. Judge was doing this largely as a favor for me. He knew nothing about the woman and had never seen her before. Among other things that the reading told her was that she had lived in Paris in a previous life and had been a courtesan and a favorite of Louis XV. It said that she should always keep about her a symbol of France—the fleur de lis.

When the reading was over, Mrs. Stern opened her purse and took out a handkerchief with a fleur de lis and disclosed that she had in her home several variations of items with designs of the fleur de lis. It was, she said, something she loved and wanted to have with her at all times. When she was fifteen years old she had been sent to school in Paris. She said that when she first went to Versailles she would anticipate what the guides were about to say. She would tell them, "Oh, the next room is the wig room."

The guide would say, "You've been here before."

But she had not been there before. Not in this lifetime. She had no idea how she knew these things. This was when she developed the desire to carry the fleur de lis.

To her the whole reading was extraordinary because it seemed to mirror her innermost instinctive desires—and memories. Yet she had gone to Virginia Beach with a skeptical attitude, to check on how right or wrong Cayce might be.

Billions of people live and die; some come back, and some do not, still others have a choice. It is a matter of deeds and misdeeds, purposes, directions, roads to be followed or retraced. We are not isolated specks in the universe. It is like a cosmic ocean, composed of many billions of drops. Each drop is both individual and a part of the infinite and each has the same ingredients as the whole ocean. It is the same thing with our souls.

The son of a vice-president of General Electric had a life reading when he was five years old. The information was given to us that he had been in his previous life a city planner and that he would be a good one now. But as the boy grew up and went to college, he showed no desire to be a city planner and, in fact, fought the whole idea.

While he was stationed in Tokyo during the war, however, he was assigned the task of handling certain matters pertaining to camp development. He did so well at this and took so much interest in it that he later became a student at Massachusetts Institute of Technology and majored in engineering. Today he is the head of a large construction firm, and city planning and development are major factors in his daily work.

In my own case, the reading gives an explanation to me for much of what I have done in my present life. My role and work with generals and other top officials in the Army, for example, according to Cayce's reading goes back to other lives, to other service, to generals under other flags of other centuries.

It is time the Occidental mind and even the organized religions of the West begin to grope seriously with these ideas—the philosophical and cosmic implications of the reincarnation concept. This too may be part of our religious rebirth!

Life readings of Cayce developed in two ways—first, in the specific lifetimes of the past and the relationships with other entities from one lifetime to another, in many cases; and, secondly, in the spiritual interpretations of individual relationships. Consider as an example an excerpt from a life reading given to Lucille.

"An entity or soul is a portion of the First Cause, or God, or Creative Energy, or the terms that may be had for the *movement* that brings matter into activity or being. Hence souls . . . have been the fruits of what? Spirit! . . . The development of the soul to the ONE purpose, the ONE CAUSE . . . to be companionate with the FIRST CAUSE!"

I remember a brother and sister who were interested in psychic phenomena. I had met the brother in a business deal in Canada; the sister worked for Western Union. They were so interested in Cayce they took a trip to Virginia Beach. Cayce gave a life reading to the sister in which he said that in a previous incarnation she had been an artist. The reading said that if she would again take some formal training she would be a successful artist in this lifetime.

Approximately six months later I had a telephone call from this young lady. She said she was having a one-man show of her pictures. She said she was selling pictures and made more with one painting than she did in a year working for Western Union. Until that reading she had never painted before in her life.

The life reading is a long journey into the past. It is almost like reading a story backward, from the present day, step by step, to the time before this. It would begin with an examination of the astrological influences of the present, those that were beneficial, those that were adverse.

From this, the steps go back and the sleeping Cayce would describe each step, each incarnation:

Of Lucille's appearance on this earth in Greece, the historical notes say of her theatrical, musical, and dancing abilities and background:

"Poyane [Lucille], time of Pliny. In the Grecian country. One of beautiful figure and gave much to the peoples in the arts of acting, for under the influence of Tacitus gained much favor from many peoples. . . . Pliny the Younger was nephew of Pliny the Elder, and came into possession of his uncle's literary love and all notes and manuscripts. . . . Close to him was the historian Tacitus—who was noted for the high moral tone of his works, though he never admitted any specific religious faith. Under these men it seems the entity has given favor and acted as a protégé in the fields of dramatic art and dancing. . . ."

Lucille checked these statements against historical records. Pliny the Younger and Tacitus were certainly contemporaries in the second half of the first century after Christ. Further, according to historical information at the New York Center for the Performing Arts, it was in the first century A.D. that women were allowed to play on the Roman stage for the first time. Moreover, with the spreading influence of Roman culture throughout the Empire, and the confrontation of Roman and Greek cultures in this period, the new customs of Romans were being imported to provinces and conquered territory throughout the Empire.

In spite of paucity of details and lack of answers to many questions that arise in the mind, this fragment of a life reading reveals a historical environment situation and time—hundreds of years past—in which all of the specifics cited in the reading could have happened.

There is beauty, there is a poetry, in the life readings, as the pattern of life itself seems to unfold in the telling.

"In the one before this we find in that period when there were settlers in the present land, and in those days there was the extending of the frontier. . . ."

This was a reading for a woman who lived in the West and it describes her immediate previous lifetime. The life reading continues after giving some detail of this immediately past life experience:

"In the one before this we find in that period when there were the returning[s] to the land of promise from captivity. During those of the second return from the Chaldean land. . . .

"In the one before this we find in that land known as the Indian in the present, and during those periods where there was the breaking up of the groups in various portions of the land, owing to the earth's tremor and the beginning of the sacred fires. . . ."

The pattern of each life reading is that of a running journey back to the beginnings, back to the First Cause, back to the primordial.

Many of the life readings would refer to the fact that the entity dwelled back in the lifetimes long since past in the land called Atlantis.

Between the theory of reincarnation and that of the lost continent of Atlantis there are bonds of historical and mystical meanings. Much has been written about Atlantis and discoveries in modern times seem to be bearing out what Cayce said in the readings. Hugh Lynn has noted that his father had not read Plato's writings on Atlantis and, so far as he or his brother Edgar Evans were aware, their father had no direct knowledge from material sources of the lost continent or the legends. If Cayce received the information from other living minds, it is one of the most remarkable examples of extra-sensory telepathy on record.

Atlantis is more than a continent that was lost; it is a theory of a civilization that has been swallowed up, a civilization that had reached physical and intellectual levels of achievement comparable to or beyond what we know today. All of this has been written about and published in many books; Cayce, however, made the contribution of giving readings on Atlantis in response to questions of individuals, and in the life readings he sometimes took the individuals back to Atlantean incarnations, approximately fifty thousand years ago. Thus Atlantis is linked closely to reincarnations. The two are truly bound together.

The first Atlantean reading I heard took place at our house, then on West Seventy-seventh Street in New York. The subject was a charming woman who was the wife of an American cartoonist. She was an aviatrix. Her reading[1] carried her back beyond present civilizations to the Atlantean period, and she was a flier (aviatrix) then, accounting for her present urge in this life. The reading said that she would prove to herself that this Atlantean story was real. It said Atlantis had reached all the way across what is now the Atlantic Ocean straight across to what is now called India, and that migrant peoples of Asia and Asia Minor may well have walked to South America. The aviatrix didn't walk but flew in her plane to the island of Bimini, and found items believed to be from the submerged continent of Atlantis. Whether these finds were later examined and evaluated by archeologists I do not not know.

Cayce gave more than twenty-five hundred life readings, and approximately seven hundred of these readings, somewhat less than half, referred to Atlantean beginnings. The wide range of the Atlantean people and activities could indicate that

[1] Reading No. 587 in the Cayce files.

such a civilization may have been fully developed, perhaps quite advanced, and involved a large number of extremely intelligent and advanced human entities.

The existence of Atlantis has long been a postulate of many thousands of people. It is the lost civilization that goes back perhaps fifty thousand years or more; it is perhaps a symbol of what could happen to all the present so-called civilization or civilizations if we abuse the laws of God and His universe.

Atlantis, as Judge gave it in the readings, would appear to be not merely a physical civilization that sank below the waves of some tremendous flood or upheaval of the earth's surface, but, rather, a link between the purely spiritual, ethereal existence and the material; as if the souls of the universe, pure and unsullied at the outset, could by their very thinking become the entity in physical form.

Whether the Atlantean story is to be accepted in physical or metaphysical terms remains unanswered. To the sleeping Cayce, drawing on the universal, it was quite real. It was a civilization that began in purity, perhaps the most pure the world has ever known, perhaps the highest. And then, as do all civilizations apparently, it fell away from the basic meanings and inescapable spiritual and, indeed, physical laws.

The reading speaks of the entities of that time and of those who lived through the periods of destruction brought on by the struggles before groups and parties and beliefs of that day:

". . . in Atlantis during periods of the breaking up . . . [the entity] . . . set sail for Egypt but ended up in the Pyrenees in what is now Portuguese, French, and Spanish lands. In Calais may still be seen the marks in the chalk cliffs of the entity's followers at attempts to create a temple activity for the followers of the Law of One. . . ."

It also states that this particular entity established the first library of knowledge "in 10,300 B.C. in what later became Alexandria in Egypt."

". . . in Atlantis when there was the breaking up of the land [entity] came to what was called the Mayan land or what is now Yucatán . . . entity was the first to cross the water in the plane or air machine of that period. . . ."

There are those who believe that nothing that we have today was not also present in the earlier civilization of Atlantis. There are those who insist that we have spent the last five thousand years or more seeking to return to that high level that Atlanteans held, to rebuild and re-create the wonders that they had and that they lost.

CHAPTER 16

Searchlight: The Association for Research and Enlightenment

The few have grown into a throng of many thousands, both at Virginia Beach and throughout the country.

The New York branch of Association for Research and Enlightenment by 1968 had grown to many hundreds of members. It was started with a handful of devoted human beings. In our homes we always made sure we had enough room to accommodate the many people who would gather for meetings, readings, lectures in connection with Cayce.

With my own business activities, which never seemed to grow more subdued or predictable, and the Cayce program and meetings, our home was a constant turmoil. Lucille handled it all in her calm and gracious way whatever the hour. Long since she had discovered—particularly in the last decade of Cayce's life—that she had not only married a large Kahn family but also a Cayce clan; when Judge and Gertrude and Gladys Davis or any and all of them came into New York, our house became almost always—and very willingly—headquarters.

There were hundreds who wanted to meet him, hundreds

who wanted readings; we had to control the times and flow of people. It was exciting; it was turbulent; it was unpredictable.

One night in New York a few years before Cayce's death, a well-known New York society woman, whose family I had known back in Kentucky, telephoned to ask if she could bring Vincent Lopez up to meet Mr. Cayce. There was a small gathering of people there at our home that evening. We told her that she and Mr. Lopez would be welcome. She said they couldn't get there until around eleven o'clock.

But when the doorbell rang, shortly after eleven, it proved to be not merely the lady and Vincent Lopez, but also the members of his orchestra. Their entrance was quite startling to this quiet group in our home, discussing metaphysics, in which, as it turned out, Mr. Lopez was deeply interested.

Lucille accepted the unexpected as part of the routine, and she handled it magnificently. Gertrude, Cayce's wife, had had an even more difficult task in Virginia Beach. She never could cook a meal or set a time for the children coming home from school to eat because people dropped in unannounced and she had to entertain them. Gertrude and Lucille had much to complain about had they wanted to—and to sympathize about. They were both serving tough masters.

Tom Sugrue was present at the first New York ARE meeting—Tom, Lucille, and myself, and a number of devoted members. We read the Bible that night and one of the readings given at Virginia Beach. And talked about the future.

Lucille, since then, has been conducting the meetings and bringing in panels of doctors, writers, psychologists, psychiatrists, and leading investigators of metaphysical phenomena for open meetings and discussions. These invariably draw an increasing number of intellectually aware, open-minded people.

Many who came into our home over these years were personalities of business, industry, the arts, government; they included authors and physicians, psychiatrists, and representatives of other disciplines.

As ARE has grown, in New York City and elsewhere, the main thrust of the work, centered in Virginia Beach, under the direction of Hugh Lynn Cayce, has become a symbol of the psychic explosion of our times. The buildings on the beach have become a center of parapsychological research. Its library has become one of the most complete and comprehensive in this field. Cayce's readings are available to association members and are cross-indexed. One of the great dreams is that the Atlantic University, chartered when Cayce was still alive, will be re-established as a great university for the study of all phases of psychic and parapsychological investigation under a faculty that will call on the most responsible leaders in these and relative fields.

With more than twelve thousand members and many more friends who support and work with the association, it has attained an outreach that today may be the opening of a whole new era of investigation that would surely fulfill in large measure Judge's own dreams and objectives.

The purposes of the national association are outlined in its official statement:

"The Association for Research and Enlightenment was incorporated under the laws of Virginia in 1931. Now a national organization, the association carried on a program based on the Edgar Cayce readings, also on the growing experience developed in study groups. The association's principal purpose is to assist its members in their study and use of its records, as they are tested in people's lives. It is not the aim of the association to develop in people the gift of seership that Edgar Cayce possessed but to help uncover the psychic awareness, the soul faculty that we have inherently, and to help apply these toward physical healing and spiritual growth.

"The Edgar Cayce legacy is at heart a body of ideals which

in his lifetime changed people's lives and is now being progressively proved as potent to do the same today. It meets human needs that more and more people are seeking to justify. It deals with questions in people's lives, leads them to probe for the answers within themselves, and to accept their own spiritual guidance.

"Above all, the association is dedicated to making practical application of the principles embodied in the Cayce readings. To this end it also cooperates with physicians who are invited to study case histories and test their patterns of treatment.

"An additional area of the association's purpose lies in promoting objective study of psychic phenomena, improving methods of distinguishing the genuine from the fraudulent, and analyzing technical information by other research organizations. . . ."

ARE is a membership organization divided into groups and committees, all functioning under the central control of the organization. The Edgar Cayce Foundation has custody of the readings and is in charge of indexing, extracting, and microfilming material in the files. The ARE Press is responsible for all publications, production and distribution of books and booklets on the material in the files and related subjects.

The heart of the association and of all Cayce activity is in Virginia Beach. Cayce's first readings on Virginia Beach came in 1920. They said this beach—there was practically nothing there at the time—was one of the most health-giving places in the world.

I recall many cases in which Judge's ideas about the therapeutic sands have been borne out.

I know how much the association, the readings of Cayce, and the work and indeed the whole aura of Virginia Beach have meant to my wife and me. I would like to quote here a statement made by Lucille about the ARE because it reflects how all of us who have been in this work for so many years feel and believe.

"The ARE," Lucille said, "seems to me to be a kind of coordinating center from many sources, merging them into a central point. When Mr. Cayce gave it the title of Association for Research and Enlightenment, I thought, oh, how perfectly dreadful a name. It was too long and clumsy—even though the original phrase was taken from a reading given at Virginia Beach. But how pertinent and wholly contemporary have these words become! What is more important today than research and enlightenment? These words meant much then—but much more now.

"We of the Association do research in many different fields of psychic phenomena. We are seeking facts—evidence built on the readings themselves. Also, and perhaps more important, this study and the practice of these teachings may induce in the individual the process of self-discovery and enlightenment, a process which may lead to changes in character, conduct, and consciousness.

"Two summers ago, in 1967, David and I went down to Virginia Beach to attend an ARE board meeting. We wanted to retrace some of the steps we had taken during all the days and years we had been there.

"We drove up to Mr. Cayce's home, the old headquarters. This is where Tom Sugrue lived when he wrote so much of *There Is a River*. We met a gentleman who said he had bought the house. He showed us around and said they had many visitors. The man had made all the fruit trees Cayce had originally planted productive again. We recalled how much Cayce loved plants and delighted in putting up his preserves, particularly figs and peach preserves.

"We were taken inside. The interior had been somewhat altered but Mr. Cayce's room was still there. The room brought back its memories of Judge. Through the windows overlooking his beloved lake—fresh water even though right next to the ocean—we remembered often seeing him whittling on a stick or fishing.

"You know, when he started to give a reading, he had to have his head in one direction for life readings and in another direction for other kinds of readings. They should investigate this, there must be some reason for it. As I remember, when he gave life readings his head was south; for physical readings it was north.

"Most of us in ARE have accepted reincarnation as a fact. If every thought, deed, and act is recorded somewhere, then we do have to meet it. It is the law of moral retribution. It will be a guide in your way of life if you can accept it.

"Tom Sugrue, who lived and wrote in that same house, had suffered but never became embittered. He accepted both intellectually and emotionally what happened to him as karmic retribution in this life. He kept his warm, outgoing personality and received much love in return. It is a beautiful thing to see—when someone can give life that much meaning. . . ."

Lucille's approach to the meaning of ARE is one of the clearest and most meaningful expressions of this work which she and I found with Tom Sugrue and so many others over so many years.

Over these same years in addition to our ARE activities I had, of course, carried on my business activities. Cayce had said to me that in the latter part of my life I would do well in the fields that drew on nature's storehouse.

I didn't understand at first. But later I became involved in a product that was in effect a fiber glass composite material. These materials, certainly, fit the description of nature's storehouse—sand and paper and glass, the products of trees, the earth, the ocean. I obtained patents covering a unique process to manufacture products using this material.

At the same time the Brunswick Radio Company has been

reactivated, and I am now involved actively in negotiations for the sale of this property to a new group anxious to have the value of Brunswick's long tradition as well as its trademark and name.

Everything in my life was built around Cayce and the readings. I have never felt that he is gone or that he left me. There is no death. It is only a learning and doing—or a not learning and not doing. The young people today, even the wildest, are seeking God in their way. They do not have to be revolutionaries to have Him. But we need centers at which we can help these young people, as ARE groups do with youth at Virginia Beach. These groups of the young who come to our headquarters include many who are amazingly gifted with rare insights. My hope is that we will be able to help them, and thousands like them, in future years.

CHAPTER 17

Interpolation

By Will Oursler

For many months I worked closely with David Kahn in the preparation of this book. It was an exhilarating experience as he poured out stories of his intimate relationships with Cayce and the Cayce family, of his own business and personal adventures, often flamboyant and brash, his encounters with leaders of American industry and business, with the White House and generals and statesmen—and with the sick and the aged and helpless who obtained help from Cayce through Dave.

All of this we recorded on tape and most of it was edited and ready for final revisions. Late in November, I told him, "Dave, we have most of the material down. It's only a matter of one or two more interviews with Lucille."

He seemed somewhat tired that day; I had, in fact, cut the interview short. Two days later he went into New York Hospital for a checkup.

We became good friends in those months of working together, and sharing so many of his life experiences, stories, goals, enterprises, victories. He still had much to do but everything was working out, he said, as Cayce had said years before it would.

Brunswick would be revived and sold, Dave insisted. Cayce had told him this in a dream only the night before. He had awakened at 3 A.M. in the same way he had always awakened in such dreams.

The fiber glass business would also work out; conferences with leading industrialists who wanted to buy his patents were about to be held. It would work out because he was following Cayce's injunction that he must, in the closing years of his life, work with material out of nature's storehouse.

Fiber glass was made of materials out of this storehouse—sand and glass, cotton and pulp paper and other cellulose components.

Even my role in helping him with the book, Dave said, was part of the pattern.

He was extremely ill in the hospital for some days. Lucille called me to tell me it was quite serious. When I saw him he seemed very weak. The old zest was almost gone. But he managed a weary smile and murmured, "I love you, Will."

It was his final good-by to a friend and associate.

Only a few days later—on December 7, 1968—Dave was dead.

But the story was not really over.

In collaboration with this writer, Lucille has set down what I consider the extraordinary and wholly unanticipated episodes of these final chapters.

BOOK THREE

For the Present . . .

"Then use those forces as are in hand and magnify His name through the world, for in so doing the entity will serve self and others, for as destructive forces have entered in . . . so must the rebuilding, resuscitating, re-establishing, reincarnated forces of the entity be manifested. . . .

"We are through for the present."

—Closing paragraphs of life reading on Edgar Cayce
in Dayton, Ohio, February 23, 1925

CHAPTER 18

A Man Called David

*By Lucille Kahn**

My husband David, as I think the story of his life and his work with Edgar Cayce indicates, was a man with an extraordinary mixture of the practical and the spiritual. He believed deeply in Judge, in the Cayce readings. He had faith in God and Biblical truth, and in brotherhood.

He believed also in survival of the soul. In his last moments of consciousness my husband, seeming to come back out of the beginnings of coma, opened his eyes and murmured to me, "Tell them—there is survival."

One series of episodes that occurred after David's passing I believe I should report. The phenomena happened and I know that Dave would want me to put down these things, whatever they may or may not imply.

Because of his own interest in Cayce, in reincarnation, in life after death, Dave on numerous occasions said, "If it is possible to break through when I make that crossing," he told me, "I'll do it."

And that was Dave too. Always certain, no matter how im-

* This chapter has been written in collaboration with Will Oursler.

possible something might appear to be, he could do it. I would ask, "Dave—how would I be sure?" And he'd say, "Don't worry, you'll all know it." It reminded me of when I was expecting my first baby and asked the gynecologist, "How will I know when to call you?" And he would give me a look and say, "You will know." That is how Dave used to say, "You'll know."

The services for my husband were held at Temple Emanu-El in New York, where he had served so many years in his work with the Men's Club. Final commitment was in Kentucky, in the bluegrass, blue-sky world in which he grew up and where he had first known and grown to love and respect the man he called Judge.

At the graveside in Kentucky, the rabbi said a few prayers in Hebrew, a few of the traditional words that are also spoken. And then, in the manner of a reading by Cayce, he said, "In the time before this, in the land of America, in the environs of Lexington, Kentucky . . . in the name of David E. Kahn."

And he went on to describe the things David had achieved in his life, in business, with the Cayce movement. And he finished these brief last words with the closing phrase that Edgar Cayce always used at the end of one of the readings: "We are through for the present. . . ."

For the present.

I have been in the parapsychological movement long enough not to be naive, not to grasp at psychic straws. I believe in the maxim that in examining such phenomena we should always seek first to find *natural* explanations. I am here, however, reporting merely facts, what happened on Tuesday when I and my son, Dick, returned by plane to New York following the services in Kentucky. Dick's wife and three children were in our house on Eightieth Street when we arrived. The lights were all on and the warmth of the lights and the greetings took some of the harshness out of coming back to our home.

The following morning, the heat came up in the house at the usual time, approximately 6 A.M. But that morning, for the first time in all the years we had shared that house, there was a crashing noise; it was as if someone had taken up a hammer and begun to beat on the pipes. The pounding was like sledgehammer blows. I had never heard anything like this before in our house. It could be heard in every room.

Dick and Judy, my daughter-in-law, were on the fourth floor. They also heard it. Sometimes it was louder than at other times. But it continued on and off all day. Judy, who is a very detached and objective individual, began to wonder about this extraordinary disturbance. "You know," she said, "sometimes you walk into a room and it starts to talk to you."

Even before Judy mentioned this, I had noticed it myself, and had wondered if it was only my imagination. As I walked from room to room, I would hear it, almost like some code against the pipes, "Boom . . . boom . . . boom . . ." It went on like that, except for moments of quiet, for the entire day.

We did make every effort to determine the cause. Dick, of course, had to go to work. Judy and I did not discuss this outbreak or indicate any undue interest in it in front of the three young children.

Dick returned from his law office around seven that evening. He was talking on the phone in the hall when a noise began in the basement so shattering I was certain the boiler was about to explode. I heard Dick say, "Please forgive me, I have to hang up." I ran down from the first floor to the basement with Dick following. I wondered how or where to turn off the gas furnace. An explosion seemed imminent. Then I saw that the washing machine was doing a jig—jumping, shaking, and screeching. This was the first time since we had been using the machine that it had acted in such a manner. As in all households, the machine had occasionally been overloaded and had needed repairs, adjustments, and small parts replaced. This time, however, I had put only a cotton blanket in it—a pair of Dave's pajamas and a few small pieces—but as it hit the last cycle it almost flew to pieces.

There are, of course, explanations for these events, but it is strangely coincidental that it all occurred the morning after we returned from Lexington, Kentucky. I keep remembering how Dave had repeatedly said it would be his intent and purpose upon passing to break through if possible, to give evidence that the personality survives bodily death. All of us (Dick, Judy, and I) were deeply impressed by these happenings and felt it was a gesture even if boisterous in the extreme.

And we said, perhaps with uncertain laughter, "All right, Dave . . . greetings. We're glad you made it. . . ."

I had the furnace man in the following morning when everything was quite normal again and I told him about the hammering that had invaded our house the day before. The furnace man said that if the water pressure builds up you can get a hammering sound. Perhaps that was the answer—although there was no indication that the pressure had built up.

When the repairman arrived, he said that the machine was unbalanced. Opening it up we discovered it was damaged inside. It was a light laundry load I had in it. But never before had such a load, or any load, light or heavy, caused the machine to do such a jig and to make such a screeching sound.

The physical explanations are perhaps entirely valid. I can accept them. Yet in twenty-three years nothing like that had happened.

On the day after those unusual occurrences, another event took place. This concerned something that began back in 1951, when Dave, the boys, and I were in Spain visiting the consul in Malaga—we were sipping a drink in the lovely gardens and Dave admired the tile-topped table depicting a bullfight. Later, the consul sent us a set of the tiles. These were used to cover the top of a chest in our liquor bar. There were enough extras to make a border of tiles on the wall behind the chest, where they had remained firmly fixed for seventeen years. On Thursday, December 12, one tile became loosened from the wall and was hanging at an angle. The 1951 trip had represented such a happy time for Dave and me. I could not, in view of the other events which took place, disassociate this also from the possibility of his attempt to communicate.

It will also be recalled that Dave had been trying to re-establish and sell the trademark and assets of the Brunswick company. Five days after his death, this was closed on satisfactory terms. It worked out, as Dave would say.

Was it merely a long series of coincidences? Dave insisted not only that he would try to break through, once he made the crossing, but also that he would try to prove survival of the personality. Somehow, he felt that on the other side there were powers that would help us to achieve what we could not do here. I am not judging this one way or the other. But what happened did happen.

Because both of us had an intimation of what might happen, in the last weeks we had together, Dave and I read Laura Huxley's book *This Timeless Moment* describing the last days and hours of her husband, Aldous Huxley. Dave and I had come to know Aldous well in the last years of his life and, through our close mutal friend, Gerald Heard, had shared his interest in mescaline and LSD. In order to alleviate the pain and to aid in the peace and understanding of his final hours, Huxley asked for and was given LSD. And to the very end Aldous Huxley was relating to his wife his thoughts, hoping he would go out fully conscious, fully in control and knowing. Laura had a tape recording machine which was recording all of this. But she had told me how difficult it was because so much of what Aldous said was lost in murmuring.

I am all for research being done with LSD for the dying if they wish it. Dave wanted desperately to tell me things but because of injections they had given him he would go off, and yet he and I both knew that he was trying to relate what he was experiencing, only to slip back, unable to find his thoughts.

I think persons who want to retain consciousness as long as humanly possible should be allowed this privilege. Dave, I knew, was angry at the drugs that kept him so groggy he was not able to communicate as he wished to, except at intervals.

Two mornings later he asked where I had been as I came in from the solarium. He said to me, "Take this down. Brunswick deal will be a big success. And my final message is this—there is a life after death."

It was as if he had had a glimpse—one glimpse—that supported his life-long faith. He wanted me to take this all down. "God is the only one, God is the father. . . ."

At another point when he had a few moments of consciousness he told me, "Take this down. I saw you sitting in a wonderful costume . . . there were jewels over you and glittering lights. And there were people all around you, worshiping you. . . ."

I said to Dave, "That was a lovely dream."

There were statements from time to time Dave tried to make, as he went in and out of this other realm. He would try to say something and his voice would fade out. He was saying only fragments of words, images.

The following morning, the nurse called early before going off night duty to say that he was still in coma. I dressed slowly. A little later my son Dick came over and I went back with him to the hospital. I knew that time was short.

Both Dick and I were familiar with the Tibetan ritual of addressing the soul as it leaves the body. The nurse went out and Dick and I were alone with Dave. I stood by Dave's bed and I said, to That which hears and was perhaps still there, "Dave, your soul is about to be liberated. You are to go in peace. You are going into the light, into God's love." I told him that all was well. I said, "Go forward, into that light. . . ."

CHAPTER 19

Journey

*By Lucille Kahn**

In 1968, leaders of the Association for Research and Enlightenment organized a proposed around-the-world trip to meet with leaders of the modern parapsychological and metaphysical movement in all parts of the world, but with particular emphasis on the Orient. Dave and I had planned to go on this trip, which was to leave from New York in February 1969. Hugh Lynn Cayce and other ARE delegates had arranged an exciting itinerary and Dave and I had been looking forward to this journey as one of the climactic experiences in our work with the ARE.

The date of the flight's departure came so close after my husband's death that I was unsure what I should do. My sons insisted that I go. Word came that they would hold a reservation for me on the Air India plane until the evening of the flight from New York and hoped that I would go.

Something compelled me to see it through.

On the day we left on our journey a memorial service was held by the New York group of ARE. It was attended by several hundred persons including the entire group who were with us on the flight.

* This chapter has been written in collaboration with Will Oursler.

The service was very moving. Many wonderful people said wonderful things about Dave, his role as a pioneer in psychical research and his achievements. Among them was Eileen Garrett, the world-famed psychic and medium. I knew that Eileen was terribly upset. When she rose to speak she cut off what she was saying rather abruptly and left the speaker's platform in tears. Unfortunately, because of the crush of people and the need to keep our schedule at the airport, I was unable to reach Eileen and see if she was all right and what had happened.

On my return to the States after our trip, I received from Eileen a carbon of a letter she had sent to Hugh Lynn about that service before we left. The letter states:

"My dear Hugh Lynn:

"I was truly embarrassed on the platform on Sunday afternoon when you so kindly asked me to speak of our good friend David Kahn.

"As soon as I began to speak I was almost 'blacked out' so to speak. I looked toward Mrs. Kahn and quite suddenly only David himself was visible. 'Look after you, Eileen,' he warned, rather in a tired way. But then he told me, 'Tell the boys to look after Lucille. She has been through a hard time and I hadn't helped much.'

"I lost sight of the audience and was overcome with emotion. I couldn't choke back the tears and was in consequence incoherent. When I went back to my seat, I heard an audible sign close to me. 'We are sending you help, so take it when it is offered.' For this reason I slipped out rather quickly. . . .

"I hope you will be good enough to let anyone who must have been disappointed with my performance know what happened to me. . . ."

We traveled not as tourists but as students on a serious quest. This was understood and recognized wherever we went.

At Dharmsala, at the foothills of the Himalayas, we spent an hour with His Holiness, the Dalai Lama. Then we crossed the holy river—the Ganges—and climbed a mile up the Himalayan mountain slope to visit the Maharishi at his ashram and to meditate in the Maharishi's gardens with the sound of the river spilling over the rocks close by.

For the purpose of visiting for a few hours with Raynor Johnson, the noted physicist who is now devoting all of his efforts to psychic studies and metaphysics, we flew three thousand miles to Sidney, Australia.

We had also been able to meet and interview a number of persons who had provided documentary evidence of past existences.

For me, one of the high moments came when we met and dined with Shanti Devi, one of the most fully documented cases of reincarnation on record. I had known and studied her story for many years and it was a most rewarding moment to be able to sit with and talk with this lovely young woman who is accepted by so many as a living proof of reincarnation. Probably no case of claimed previous existence has ever been examined so carefully by modern evidential techniques.

She was a child when she made incredible yet completely verified identifications of a past experience. That was many years ago. She is a charming lady who teaches Hindi in the schools of New Delhi and who wants to give all her time to teaching Yoga and meditation. There was a great rapport between Shanti Devi and me. She gave me a mantra (prayer or chant) to use in my own meditations.

My interest in reincarnation had grown out of my involvement with the Cayce movement when I met Dave in New York City. Both Dave and I found, after long study of the readings, that we could accept this concept because it was so reasonable. It explained the inequities of life. The life readings of young children of relatives and friends invariably spoke of urges and talents from previous lives and how these with proper training should become guides in the present. Over the years we observed the accuracy of these statements as we followed these children into their professions in adulthood.

All of the experiences of the journey helped to build and reinforce my beliefs in this theory that we live and live again until the soul has rid itself of all desires—all attachments. I have been held by the symbolic imagery of Buddhism in which reincarnation is likened to the flame of a candle. As the candle begins to flicker and burn out, the dying flame of one lights the candle of the next time to come. The soul carries on as the flame. The body—the candle—is used up and gone. But the flame does not die. This is the light, the memory, the continuity, the soul, the eternal glow of being itself.

This concept of continuity, of the flame that does not die, brings me back to the earlier experience that took place in London, our first stop after leaving New York.

On the day after we arrived there, a symposium was held with a number of the most noted spiritualists in England, including Ronald Beasley, Harry Edwards, Ursula Roberts, and Ena Twigg, the medium who worked with the late Bishop James Pike on his reported communications with his late son.

The symposium lasted all day. At the end of this prolonged and animated discussion, Ena Twigg was asked by a member whether she would give a reading to someone who had recently lost her husband. She consented knowing nothing of my background.

I agreed willingly to go with her. Another member of our group, Dr. Herbert Puryear, an American psychologist, went with me—also Ruben Miller, another of the group. We went in fact to Ruben Miller's hotel room for this reading.

Mrs. Twigg is a birdlike woman, in her middle years, I would judge. She sat before me and she put her head to one side in a listening position.

Then it appeared someone was speaking whom she could hear. She said, "I heard you. He passed quickly. . . . He was a man of high integrity and truth. He knew Cayce before this organization was developed. He was methodical in writing. . . ."

Mrs. Twigg appeared to be serving here as an intermediary between us the living and those on the other side. We could not always be sure she was talking to us or to them. Then there was a statement from Dave: "I want to tell you, darling. It's a hundred per cent true. . . ."

This was Dave. The voice was Ena Twigg but the words were Dave, in my mind. And yet I had not decided what it was that was happening or what it meant. Again, his words in her voice: "You are a cornerstone of the foundation."

Then it was Ena Twigg telling me, "He is saying he is glad he didn't have a regular funeral. Something about a daughter like you to look at. Then he seems to say, 'You have come here to find me.'" She added a moment later, "He is highly intuitive. I am getting Dad or Dave. Who is Dave?"

There followed more direct quotes from Dave. "Don't cry. This is God's work in action. I'll never let you go. I am helping you put the papers together."

Ena Twigg stated that "he left a helluva muddle on paper work." (This was certainly true.)

An instant later, it was Dave speaking directly through her, although there was no voice change, of course: "The responsibility is not for you to take on for yourself. Delegate it. . . . Get somebody else to help you. . . ."

Then Ena Twigg, speaking for him, "You kept his signet ring. (I did.) He showed me a chain with a medallion on it. You were not there when he died. (True.) After he died you came and stood at the foot of his bed. . . ." (I did.)

Much of what she had been saying, and what Dave had been saying, had been close to complete accuracy, although there were one or two errors or question marks. But these last statements were exact and startling because they were things that it seemed utterly impossible for her to have known. For example, that I was not in the room when Dave died. I had been sitting with Dick in the hospital solarium that morning and my son David rushed in to say one word, "Come."

It was then I went in and stood by his bed.

Yet Ena Twigg was very precise and very certain on this point and she was correct.

Dave was speaking again through Ena Twigg: "I want to tell you something. Immediately when I was finished with my body I thought I must get back to tell them it is true. . . ."

He then said something about, "I made you laugh. . . . I feel tremendous energy. . . . I don't want things to fade away."

Ena Twigg then mentioned the name Nellie and finally Ellie. Ellie was Eleanor—Dave's youngest sister and his special favorite. He always called her Ellie, not Eleanor.

It was at this point that the reading took a dramatic turn. It must be remembered that this reading took place in London, that most of the things she said, or Dave apparently said through her, were things that it would be very difficult for her to know or to have obtained through someone close; the precise details were simply too petty and unimportant.

Moreover, I had told only three or four people of the experiences in our home on the day after Dave died. One of these was Will Oursler. Dick and Judy knew about it also; they were part of it. And I think one of our neighbors. I told no one on the trip. That was all.

It is highly unlikely that any of these persons would have communicated this information to Ena Twigg three thousand miles away in England, on the chance that I would go on the trip and would be at the London symposium or get a reading from Ena Twigg.

It was here that the whole matter of what happened at the house in New York came into the picture.

The question was raised: How had he tried to break through? And the words: "Tried to do something at home . . . noise . . . helluva noise. . . ." And Ena Twigg then said, "Trying to relay what they are saying. . . ."

Then it was Dave again, communicating through Ena Twigg: "I tried to move something in your bedroom. I tried to appear to you. Would you be surprised if you saw me?" Now Ena Twigg had placed her hands on the table beside her. She said something about getting a name. And she said, "Noise . . . noise . . . something being moved. Noise attached to movement. Moving. Noise . . . noise . . . noise. . . ."

While she was saying this it was as if she were hearing the noise and the commotion; her whole expression reacted; her hands seemed to be trying to hold the table down physically, as though she were sure it would bound up if she removed her hands.

"Bang . . . bang . . . bang," she said. And added the words, "Trying to make my name. . . ." (This was possibly a direct quote from Dave and might refer to what had seemed to me to be the codelike hammer sounds.)

At this point I asked, "What was he trying to prove?"

There was a burst of laughter from the others at my question. Then he was speaking directly through Ena Twigg again, "To prove I was there. When you go back restart with psychic activities. Promise me now that you will . . . trying to give you a personal experience. This is the breakthrough, watch the next step. . . ."

Ena Twigg added to this, "He says he doesn't know where we will meet again. And he says he notices 'You still like pretty clothes.'"

I did not know then, and do not know now, what all of this experience means.

I do know that the words and phrases were his, they

were his way of thinking and speaking; I know also that the meanings were his, and I know that the incidents described reflected precisely what had happened. The notes of this entire experience were taken down by Dr. Herbert Puryear.

I know that these were facts and that somehow they had been carried across thousands of miles, this minutia of the living and dying, details and trivia that seemed too small to pay attention to or even to try to guess.

Throughout our later years together, I repeat, because it is important, Dave told me many times that if there were a way to break through he would do it. It was a challenge to him; he wanted to prove that it could be achieved, that if survival after death was indeed a fact he would find a way to let us know.

I cannot say for sure.

But it seems very possible that he did.

CHAPTER 20

Epilogue

By Will Oursler

This story of a man named Cayce and a man named David Kahn, as told by Dave and finished by his wife, is really an unfinished story. The meaning of what he put down here, and what he wanted to say, is that all the Cayce work is real and true; that there is survival, that there is the life before and the life to follow, that there is the glowing beauty and splendor of the universe of which we are eternally a part.

His meaning was a reaffirmation of his faith in life and in the simple things that make it up. He was not perfect nor did he pretend to be. He enjoyed the excitement of business and battle and victory, all of the rough competitive struggle of the business world.

But his guide, his meaning, his direction, his world, everything he knew and did, was oriented toward that strange and wonderful friend of his, who walked into his home one day, more than half a century ago.

Judge would sometimes say, "I don't know what I am doing. I only know it is helping people, it is saving lives. It is bringing meaning to other lives. It is God's work. . . ."

This was the man—Edgar Cayce—Dave served through all those incredible, wonderful years of their lives.